Produced for the Politics Association
Old Hall Lane
Manchester M13 0XT

Sheffield Hallam University Press
Learning Centre
City Campus
Howard Street
Sheffield S1 1WB

Designed and typeset by
Design Studio, Learning Centre, Sheffield Hallam University

© 2000
ISBN 0 86339 873 1

 *Sheffield Hallam University*

Britain and the European Union:
an Uneasy Partnership

by Duncan Watts

About the author

Duncan Watts is the current Editor of the Politics Association Resource Centre. Formerly a Head of Department in both Grammar and Comprehensive Schools, he has wide experience of teaching and examining in Modern History and Government and Politics. He is now involved in some part-time tutoring at 'A' Level, but much of his time is spent in writing books and articles on areas of Modern Political Development. Among other works, he has written two volumes in the *Introducing* series published by Sheffield Hallam University Press, and he is the editor-in-chief of this set of books, *Politics 2000*.

Acknowledgement

The author and SHU Press wish to express their deep gratitude to June Burnham who kindly agreed to check the draft version of this book for any inaccuracies present in the text. Her task was meticulously performed and her comments both encouraging and stimulating.

Titles available in this series:

October 1999
British Government and Politics: a Comparative Guide (core text)
January 2000
British Electoral Systems: Achieving a Sense of Proportion
British Voters: the Changing Basis of Party Choice
Parliament in an Age of Reform
The Changing Constitution: Evolution or Revolution?
Whitehall and the Civil Service: Issues for the Millennium and Beyond

Contents

Introduction

The war of 1939-1945 was a disaster that brought much discredit upon the old international order. For many Europeans, the hostilities called the very idea of the nation state into question. After all, in a continent of sovereign countries, France and Germany had been in armed conflict three times in less than a hundred years, twice as part of major world confrontations. Other countries had been drawn into the struggle, whatever their reservations. By 1945, Europe was seriously weakened, and the task of organising recovery was urgent.

Such was the background to the unveiling of the Schuman Plan in the summer of 1950. The gist of his proposal was for a pooling of Franco-German production of coal and steel. But his purpose went far beyond this immediate goal. As he put it:

The solidarity in production thus established will make it plain that any war between France and Germany becomes not merely unthinkable, but materially impossible...this proposal will build the first concrete foundations of a European federation which is indispensable to the preservation of peace...

The establishment of the European Coal and Steel Community in 1951 was an attempt to achieve unity by mutual consent rather than by force, and because of its success the six nations involved decided to further their experiment. The Treaty of Rome (1957) which brought about this development was a landmark in postwar Europe, for it created a 'Common Market' in which the members were prepared to sacrifice some of their economic independence in the cause of a closer economic and political harmonisation.

After a difficult period in the early 1980s, the impetus was renewed by the passing of the Single European Act of 1986 which not only planned to remove all remaining technical and fiscal restrictions on trade, but began the process leading to full monetary and economic union. By the end of 1992,

1

there was to be a 'Europe without frontiers'. Barriers between member-states were progressively removed so that, among other things, people can now live and work where they choose, and industrialists can sell their products anywhere in the European Community on the basis of harmonised standards. A series of accompanying measures ensured that academic qualifications, and diplomas in careers ranging from nursing to hairdressing, are acceptable across the EU.

Under the arrangements negotiated at Maastricht, 1991, detailed work was done to prepare for a single currency, along with the planned creation of a European Bank; a Social Chapter was added to ensure that the Community developed a social dimension as well as an economic one. In January 1999, the single currency was in operation in eleven countries, members believing that it would pave the way for steady growth, and insulate them from the turmoil still reverberating throughout the world's financial markets. Using one currency, they hoped, would make companies more competitive and benefit consumers by providing them with lower prices.

Ultimately, however, the members of the European Community - especially those in the fast lane - have embarked upon more than this, for the Treaty of Rome envisaged that political unity would come about through economic co-operation. As a result of the ratification of the Maastricht Treaty, the Community has now become a European Union, and this marks a new phase in the history of European unification.

The process developed over 40 years has not been without its setbacks and crises, for each member-country is inevitably watchful of its own interests, and anxious to preserve its best traditions. Each step forward has had to be painfully negotiated. Yet, however slow at times the progress has been, the direction in which 'The Six' (and now 'The Fifteen') were moving, has never been in doubt. One of the founding fathers of the Community, Robert Schuman, shrewdly observed that Europe would not be created 'at a stroke or according to a single plan'. It would be built through solid achievements.

The European Union has been a distinctive creation. There have been several examples of countries which have joined up with one another in ventures of mutual benefit, but in aim, method and achievement this one has gone much further than the others. The Union has been more than just a customs union; it has aimed for an ever-closer-union of its peoples. It developed supra-national institutions with powers binding upon its members and it has been more successful than its rivals. Its steady enlargement - with other nations still queuing up to join - points to its health and vitality.

Britain and the European Union

Since 1973, Britain has been part of the EC, but the relationship has been an uneasy one. For many years, we stood by and watched from the outside. Our attitude was expressed by Winston Churchill, whose often pro-European rhetoric has been an inspiration to many pro-Europeans today: 'We are linked, but not comprised...we are with Europe, but not of it'.

Now, we are part of it, but journalists, politicians and others still agonise over our precise commitment. Attitudes in Britain range from the fervently pro-European ('Euro-fanatics'), who believe that Britain must become more European in outlook and do not shrink from the political commitment this involves, to the outright opponents of closer ties who feel either that we should never have joined or that we have gone as far as we need to, for 'enough is enough'. These 'Euro-phobes' or 'Euro-sceptics' stress Britain's need to cling to its sovereign power. In between, there are many who accept the fact of membership, who feel that on balance it is beneficial and believe that Britain would be isolated and exposed outside the Union, but have doubts about surrendering further powers to Brussels ('Euro-agnostics').

Coming to terms with a reduced status in the world has not been easy for Britain, and discussion of Britain's position has aroused passionate dispute at Westminster and been the cause of sharp division within both main parties. The pro-Europeans have been encouraged by the steps The Fifteen have recently taken, whereas others see these moves as a serious erosion of our sovereignty. In her Bruges Speech, Margaret Thatcher showed the parameters of her vision of Europe, when she spoke of 'willing and active co-operation between individual states' as 'the best way to build a successful European Community'. In France, General de Gaulle was a powerful exponent of a similar view, and many British people tend to say 'thus far, and no farther'.

In Britain, there is a great deal of talk about independence and sovereignty, though in the last 40 years much of this has been whittled away. Some commentators like to talk of Parliament as the supreme decision-making body, but in reality its supremacy has been greatly impaired by the Treaty of Accession in 1972, by the Single European Act and (for a time) by membership of the Exchange Rate Mechanism in 1990. There is still some reluctance to accept that when we embarked upon closer involvement with Europe in 1972, we took a far-reaching constitutional step, for the EU does not just offer advice, it can and does produce and enforce obligations upon its member-countries. The only ultimate expression of Parliamentary Sovereignty left untouched is the right that Britain has to withdraw from the Union.

Such implications of membership are becoming ever more apparent, not just upon our constitutional arrangements, but upon the attitudes of political parties and the fortunes of politicians. Life in the Union affects our daily lives, for the decisions taken in Brussels touch upon so many areas of activity, from the purity of our water-supplies to regional aid, from workers' rights to consumer protection. Britain has a voice, one of twelve, in drawing up such proposals, but as their impact is felt back at home, many people have been confirmed in their doubts. Whereas other countries cannot understand why the British feel so troubled by membership and see us as a country which always say 'No, No, No!', at home there is a lack of enthusiasm and commitment confirming our reputation as Reluctant Europeans. It is with this in mind that we proceed to examine the relationship of Britain and Europe in the postwar era, and describe it as An Uneasy Partnership.

Background information

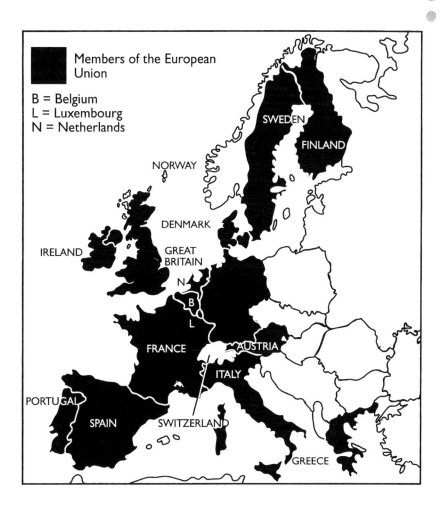

Members of the European Union

B = Belgium
L = Luxembourg
N = Netherlands

SWEDEN

FINLAND

NORWAY

DENMARK

IRELAND

GREAT
BRITAIN

N

B

L

FRANCE

AUSTRIA

ITALY

PORTUGAL

SPAIN

SWITZERLAND

GREECE

A profile of the Union

Key dates

1950	Schuman Declaration
1951	Treaty of Paris, setting up ECSC
1952	ECSC in operation
1955	Messina talks on further economic integration
1957	Treaties of Rome, setting up EEC and Euratom
1958	EEC and Euratom in operation
1962	Common Agricultural Policy agreed and in operation
1967	Merger Treaty; ECSC, EEC and Euratom combine to form EC
1973	Accession of Denmark, Ireland and United Kingdom
1975	Lome Convention agreed and in operation
1979	EMS in operation
	Direct elections to European Parliament
1981	Accession of Greece
1985	Withdrawal of Greenland
1986	Accession of Portugal and Spain
1990	Accession of East Germany
1991	Maastricht Treaty (TEU)
1993	Ratification of Maastricht, establishing European Union
1995	Accession of Austria, Finland and Sweden
1996	Intergovernmental Conference
1997	Amsterdam Summit

The member states

Country	Accession date	Population (millions)
Austria	1995	8.0
Belgium	1958	10.1
Denmark	1973	5.2
Finland	1995	5.0
France	1958	58.0
German	1958*	81.5
Greece	1981	10.4
Ireland	1973	3.5
Italy	1958	57.2
Luxembourg	1958	0.4
Netherlands	1958	15.4
Portugal	1986	9.9
Spain	1986	39.1
Sweden	1995	8.8
United Kingdom	1973	58.2

Total population = 370.7m (October 1995)

NB * *German unification occurred on October 3, 1990; before that, references to Germany allude to West Germany.*

Current membership of the European economic and political organisations

EU/EFTA members	Council of Europe	EFTA	EU	OECD
Austria	•		•	•
Belgium	•		•	•
Denmark	•		•	•
Finland	•		•	•
France	•		•	•
German	•		•	•
Greece	•		•	•
Iceland	•	•		•
Ireland	•		•	•
Italy	•		•	•
Liechtenstein	•	•		
Luxembourg	•		•	•
Netherlands	•		•	•
Norway	•	•		•
Portugal	•		•	•
Spain	•		•	•
Sweden	•		•	•
Switzerland	•	•		•
United Kingdom	•		•	•
Non-EU/EFTA				
Albania	•			
Andorra	•			
Bulgaria	•			
Croatia	•			
Cyprus	•			
Czech Republic	•			
Estonia	•			
Hungary	•			
Latvia	•			
Lithuania	•			
Malta	•			
Moldova	•			
Poland	•			
Rumania	•			
Russia	•			
San Morino	•			
Slovakia	•			
Solvenia	•		•	
The former Yugoslav Republic of Macedonia	•			

Turkey	•		•
Ukraine	•		
Non-European Countries			
Australia			•
Canada			•
Japan			•
Mexico			•
New Zealand			•
USA			•
Total	40	4	15	25

The EU budget

Income is derived from four main sources:
i   Customs duties on products imported from outside the EU
ii Agricultural levies charged at the external frontiers of the EU to bring
    the price of imported foodstuffs from the rest of the world up to the levels
    of the Union
iii A proportion of the VAT collected in the member states, calculated
    according to a uniform assessment procedure. For countries such as
    Greece, Ireland, Portugal and the UK, where private consumption is a
    larger share of national wealth, a limit is set of 55% of the total VAT base
iv The so-called 'fourth-resource', created in 1988; this is based on the GNP
    of member states and therefore the figure helps to ensure that what is
    contributed is in accordance with the ability of countries to pay

NB. At the Berlin Summit, March 1999
•   the emphasis was switched from financing the EU from i and iii (ii is a
    relatively small feature of Union income) to item iv.
•   Britain was allowed to retain its rebate won at Fontainebleau in 1984
    (see p 39)
•   As part of a new look at imbalances in net contributions which had
    become unsustainable, the Austrians, Dutch, Germans and Swedes will
    contribute less in future as a proportion of EU income, whilst Denmark,
    France and Italy will pay more.
•   See pp 146 for more details of the contributions and benefits received by
    member countries.

Expenditure goes primarily on:

- Support for farm prices, including reduction of stocks
- Structural funds
- Joint action in matters relating to energy, environment, industry, research and transport
- Co-operation with Third World countries
- Co-operation with the countries of Central and Eastern Europe
- Administrative expenditure

NB. The pattern of expenditure has changed considerably in recent years. When Britain joined the Community, 80.6% of spending went on agriculture and fisheries policy. The figure agreed at Berlin for the years until 2006 was 46%.

Glossary of relevant terminology

Additionality	The principle that EU aid should be additional to spending by the national governments, and not substitute for it
Benelux	Belgium, Holland and Luxembourg
CAP	Common Agricultural Policy
CFSP	Common Foreign and Security Policy
Cohesion	Action to reduce regional differences within the EU, brought about by structural funds to boost living conditions
Common Market	Original name for tariff-free area of The Six
Communautaire	Supportive of the principles of the European Union
Convergence	The idea that the economic performance of EU nations must be brought more closely into line before full economic and monetary union can be achieved
Democratic Deficit	The lack of democracy and accountability in the decision-making processes of the EU
ECSC	European Coal and Steel Community
EDC	European Defence Community
EEA	The name given to the bloc of 18 EU and EFTA countries; Switzerland did not join
EFTA	European Free Trade Area
Euro	The new name for the single currency

Eurocorps   A mainly Franco-German brigade (plus Benelux and Spain) established in 1993 as a fighting force; operational from 1995

Federal   Strictly speaking, a division of responsibility in which power is divided between one central authority which tackles some issues such as foreign policy and defence, and several states or provinces which deal with other matters. In an EU context, it is often used as a description for policies leading in the direction of closer European integration

Intergovernmental Conference   A conference summoned by member states with the intention of amending EU treaties

QMV   Qualified Majority Voting

SEA   Single European Act

Subsidiarity   Refers to the limits of Community action; the idea that functions should be carried out at the lowest appropriate level

Supranationalism   This implies the transfer of some national sovereignty to a multi-national organisation which acts on behalf of all the countries involved - e.g., from Britain to the EU

Transparency   EU jargon for opening-up the institutions of the EU to the public gaze; more openness in decision-making

Treaty of Rome   In March, 1957, six nations signed this Treaty establishing the European Economic Community

Post-war cooperation in Europe, 1945-1973

INTRODUCTION

The idea of a united Europe has a long history, its origins dating back to at least the time of the Holy Roman Empire. Attempts have been made in the last two centuries to unite the continent by force, under first Napoleon and then Hitler, but they were unsuccessful. More peaceful schemes have been advanced, with proposals for a Pan-European Union and a common market being made in 1923. However, it was the failure of the Fuhrer's bid to dominate Europe which proved to be the inspiration for a new initiative.

World War Two was a catastrophe which discredited the old international order and for many Europeans the basic ingredient of that order, the independent nation-state. By 1945 many people saw that it was the time to lay aside the old rivalries and create new bonds of cooperation and friendship between Germany and the other countries. In particular, it was necessary to ensure that France and Germany should live and work together in peaceful cooperation, for they had been at war three times in less than one hundred years.

This chapter tells the story of the early attempts to achieve greater harmony and unity in Europe, and of Britain's reaction to the moves towards European integration.

ASK YOURSELF

• What do you think was the main reason for close cooperation in Western Europe?
• Why were the major developments in the economic rather than the political field?

- Why did Britain stand aloof from many of the integrationist schemes?
- Why were the efforts of The Six successful in achieving an effective union, whereas alternative schemes such as EFTA failed to make much impact?
- Why was Britain initially rebuffed and eventually successful in its bid to join the EEC?

MAIN TEXT

Early moves

Since 1945, there has been economic, political and military co-operation between the countries of Western Europe as never before in peacetime. It has been encouraged by the United States and was for much of the period stimulated by fear of the Soviet Union, for soon after World War Two it became apparent that the main threat to Western Europe came from the USSR rather than from Germany. Unity might give more security.

Initially, the German problem was one which had to be addressed. Any movement in the direction of unity could not preclude German involvement. If there was close cooperation in Western Europe, then this might help to contain German strength. A later British Prime Minister much interested in developments on the continent, Harold Macmillan, noted this at the time: 'The most important motive behind the movement for European integration is the need to attach Germany permanently to Western Europe, but in such a manner that she cannot dominate it. This is as much a British as a continental interest. After all, we have fought two wars about this in one generation'. He realised the importance of Germany's position in Europe, and like other forward-looking politicians of the era recognised that it was a key barrier against the potential threat posed by the Soviet Red Army.

Beyond these important tactical considerations, however, there were other factors. After many wars, there tends to be a mood of idealism, a feeling that the horrors of war must never be allowed to haunt the world again. This happened after World War Two, and especially it was felt that there was a need to end the historic rivalry of France and Germany by linking the two nations in some larger organisation. A 'European Idea' developed, the idea of a strong, independent and prosperous Europe.

Indeed, a major reason for moves towards European unity was the appaling destruction in Europe. The failure of nation states in the past (many had collapsed in the period 1920-1945) and the weakness of those remaining at the end of the war, meant that there was an urgent need to bring together the states and peoples of Europe in some new organisation, in the hope that the calamities of bygone days might be overcome. In 1945, the continent was devastated, France, Germany and Italy being reduced to chaos; their people were often out of work, sometimes starving or homeless, always poor. Economic life had been disrupted, and great human suffering caused. Common action, it was believed, might help industry and agriculture to recover.

There was, then, in 1945 and the years immediately following, a most unusual willingness to think in European rather than in national terms, helped by the fact that politicians such as Adenauer in West Germany, De Gasperi in Italy and Monnet and Schuman in France were, in varying degrees, internationalists. If reconstruction was their immediate goal, they also realised the need for this to be underpinned by peace in Europe. Without this, economic recovery would merely serve to fuel the engines of future war. European leaders, therefore, had to address themselves to twin tasks:
i. How to promote economic recovery and provide a decent standard of living for the people of Europe.
ii. How to bring about reconciliation so that old hatreds would not resurface, and move forward by creating a new political stability on the continent.

In the search for this constructive co-operation, it was hoped that progress might follow in the three broad areas to which we have already referred.

Military cooperation after 1945

Soon after the war ended, the Western Powers saw more danger from the USSR than from a resurgent Germany, and many statesmen saw the need to create a military framework to complement other arrangements for the rebuilding of Europe. The Soviet Union had an armed forces estimated at 4 million and she was credited with possessing 6000 planes; this represented an enormous superiority over the military resources of the West. The surly attitude of the Russian leaders under Stalin, the Berlin Blockade and the seizure of Czechoslovakia served to confirm fears in England and France that there was a 'red menace' in the East of the continent.

15
• • •

In 1948, Britain, France and the Benelux countries signed the **Pact of Brussels,** a vague commitment to set up a joint defensive system. Its military significance was overshadowed by the establishment of the **North Atlantic Treaty Organisation (NATO)**, in 1949. The governments of the USA, Canada and the West European nations agreed that 'an armed attack against one or more of them in Europe or North America (should) be considered an attack against them all', and consequently that they would take such action as was necessary 'including the use of armed force' to cope with any such act of aggression.

In 1955, following the failure of 'The Six' to create a European Defence Community (see p28), the **Western European Union (WEU)** was formed. It was an enlargement of the Brussels Pact to include Italy and Germany, and was designed to ensure the better coordination of defence arrangements between the signatories.

Political cooperation

This was for a long while less marked than cooperation in the military or economic field. The **Council of Europe** was set up in 1949, to serve primarily as a forum for parliamentary opinion. It was a debating body, lacking in legislative or executive power, and it did and does not discuss such matters as defence policy. It promotes cultural bonds between member nations. The Council was responsible for drawing up the *Convention on Human Rights and Fundamental Freedoms*, which imposed obligations on all signatory powers. Coming into force in 1953, the Convention obliged members to promote human rights and to recognise that individuals possess them under international law.

Of course, a major purpose of the statesmen who created the European Economic Community was to promote closer political union, though in its early years this aspect of its work was secondary to economic goals. Similarly, the WEU was a political, as well as a military union.

Economic cooperation

In July 1947, Belgium, the Netherlands and Luxembourg reached an agreement to form a customs union, and thereafter they became known as the **BENELUX** countries. The success of their venture encouraged further cooperation.

By 1947, the West European economies were beginning to recover, helped by the assistance given by the United States through the Marshall Plan. It was necessary to create an organisation to supervise the administration of this relief, and early in the following year a number of countries came together in the **Organisation for European Economic Cooperation (OEEC)**. The Soviet Union's satellites were invited to join, but did not do so. (NB: In 1961, the OEEC was replaced by a new body with much greater geographical scope, the **Organisation for Economic Cooperation and Development (OECD)**. All the major industrial countries of what used to be known as the 'free world' are members, including the United States and Japan).

The major step forward was Schuman's declaration in May 1950, proposing a **European Coal and Steel Community (ECSC)**. The French Foreign Minister announced that 'it is no longer the moment for vain words, but for a bold act - a constructive act'. He set out a plan which was really the brain child of Jean Monnet, to establish a new body to manage all coal and steel production in Germany and France, an organisation open to all other European countries. The aim was to create a tariff-free market in which there would be no customs barriers to restrict trade in coal and steel across Western Europe. As Hugo Young has written[1]: 'It proposed the boldest fusing of the resources and interests of two great nations that modern Europe had ever seen'.

Two points stand out in the Schuman Declaration. First, it was recognised that it was necessary to move towards greater unity on the continent by degrees, as it says by concentrating at first on a 'limited but decisive point'. Secondly, immediate action could begin on the basis of cooperation between two countries alone, and he was talking of France and Germany. This was effectively the beginning of that Franco-German axis which has been so important in European affairs ever since. Schuman was clear about the road he was taking:

The contribution which an organised and active Europe can make to civilisation is indispensable for the maintenance of peaceful relations. France, by championing during more than twenty years the idea of a united Europe, has always regarded it as an essential objective to serve the cause of peace. Because Europe was not united, we have had war.
A united Europe will not be achieved all at once, nor in a single framework; it will be formed by concrete measures which first of all create a solidarity in fact. The uniting of the European nations requires that the age-old opposition

between France and Germany be overcome; the action to be taken must - first of all - concern France and Germany.

Monnet later recorded[2] his thoughts in his Memoirs:
The Schuman proposals are revolutionary or they are nothing...The indispensable first principle of these proposals is the abnegation [renunciation] of sovereignty in a limited but decisive field...Any plan which does not involve this indispensable first principle can make no useful contribution to the solution of the grave problems that face us. Cooperation between nations, while essential, cannot alone meet our problem. What must be sought is a fusion of the interests of the European peoples, and not merely another effort to maintain an equilibrium of those interests...

The French asked six countries to participate in discussions. Britain declined the invitation, but West Germany, Italy and the Benelux countries accepted and went on to sign the Treaty of Paris in April 1951, by which basic production of raw materials was to be pooled. It began its work in 1952, and this marks the foundation of serious economic union in Europe. Indeed, the launch of the ECSC marks the beginning of the European Community which today we know better as the European Union. Yet from the start of the European adventure, the pioneers of European cooperation had an agenda other than economic. Their goal was political union. The Preamble of the draft Coal and Steel Community was explicit, in saying that the six governments:
Resolved to substitute for historic rivalries a fusion of their essential interests, and to establish, by creating an economic community, the foundation of a broad and independent community among peoples long divided by bloody conflicts, and to lay the bases of institutions capable of giving direction to their future common destiny...

The success of the ECSC inspired The Six to extend their cooperation over the whole area of economic activity, and at the Messina Conference in 1955 they decided to examine the possibility of a general economic union, and the development of the peaceful use of atomic energy. In 1957, the ministers of The Six established **EURATOM**, and by signing the main **Treaty of Rome** set up the **European Economic Community (EEC)**; both organisations came into operation in January 1958. It is to the EEC initiative that we must shortly turn. However, there is one other economic organisation in Western Europe, the **European Free Trade Area (EFTA)**, which was formed at this time.

Britain tried to persuade The Six to join with them in a wider association of countries which could then work towards customs-free trade in industrial goods. The Six turned down the proposals, but Britain and six other nations of the OEEC went ahead in 1960; their creation, EFTA, was a looser group within which all tariffs on industrial goods were to be abolished by 1970. These two economic groupings of Western Europe, the EEC and EFTA, became known as the *Inner Six* and the *Outer Seven*.

Members of the European Free Trade Association

Members of the European Economic Community

The development of the European Community, 1958-1973

The Rome Treaty set out major objectives for The Six, including:
* establishing a customs union, in which all internal barriers to trade would be removed, and a common external tariff applied to the outside world
* developing a common agricultural policy
* harmonising social security arrangements
* providing for the free movement of labour and capital
* developing regional and social funds to assist poorer areas of their territory to produce new products and retrain workers whose skills became obsolete.

With the fulfilment of these objectives, there would be a 'Common Market' comprising the three elements, the ECSC, the EEC and Euratom. The term is in a sense misleading, for it has a narrow focus, implying a customs union plus a greater degree of internal market freedom than that achieved simply by removing tariff barriers. While this was certainly established by the Treaty, the concept of economic unity underlying it is a broader one. As Article 2 explained, the Six were aiming for

a harmonious development of economic activities, a continuous and balanced expansion, an increased stability, an accelerated raising of the standard of living, and closer relations between its member states.

The Common Market was a means to this end, not the end in itself. The aim of the Rome Treaty was economic unity. It does not directly mention political unity, but it is quite impossible to divorce economics from politics in this context. Governments are by their nature political and decisions on economic matters cannot be made without taking political considerations into account. The Founding Fathers of the EEC were well aware of this, and knew that there were clear political implications in the treaty they had signed. Yet on this occasion their language was rather less grandiloquent than it was in the Treaty of Paris. There was no talk of 'merging interests' or 'sharing destiny', although the Six 'were determined to lay the foundations of an ever closer union among the peoples of Europe'.

A few years later, the President of the EEC Commission pointed the way forward, when he observed[3]:

The rest is for the future and by the rest I mean common foreign and defence policies and, in addition, the crowning of all our endeavours by a political arrangement that will embrace them all.

Progress after the signing of the Rome Treaty

The establishment of the EEC was in many respects a decisive moment in post-war history. The Six had continued with their earlier resolve to create integration along the lines of supra-national activity, and in creating the new organisation they were on this occasion covering a much wider area of policy than in the ECSC. Clearly, within the countries involved there was developing a momentum for greater cooperation, and this was based firmly upon the strong axis linking France and Germany. The historic discord between the two nations which British policy-makers had always taken for granted was at an end, and now Britain was off-stage in the evolution of West European integration.

In 1967, the three independent organisations (the ECSC, the EEC and EURATOM) were merged into a single **European Community (EC)**, with the Commission based in Brussels, the Parliament in Strasbourg and the Court of Justice in Luxembourg. The merger of separate national markets into a large single unit could not be achieved immediately, but it was proposed that the transition period should be over by 1970.

In fact, progress was ahead of schedule, for members recognised that there was less likelihood of success if they all pursued divergent economic policies. A Common Agricultural Policy (CAP) was agreed in 1962, all customs duties between The Six were eliminated in 1968, and by then a common external tariff was applied to goods from outside the Community. In other fields, such as transport, industrial and social policies, progress was less impressive. However, by the late 1960s/early 1970s, discussions began on ways of moving towards political and monetary union, though they were at this stage inconclusive.

Quickly, 'big businesses' and especially large, multi-national corporations benefited, and many mergers took place. In the first five years, the GNP of the Community rose 27%, as compared with 18% for the USA and 14% for Britain, and statistics for industrial production were similarly impressive.

American investment in Europe, especially in technology, quickly developed, and trade within the Community was considerably expanded. In fact, the years up to the early 1970s were good ones for The Six. During that time, industrialists benefited from the large market of about 170m people, and West Germany, especially, prospered via its membership. The Franco-German axis was a strong one; two traditional enemies had buried their differences, and were working in a mutually beneficial harmony.

Up until 1969, General de Gaulle dominated the Community, and he used France's veto to block Britain's attempts to join. British governments, Labour and Conservative, had come to be impressed by the progress of The Six which in the early years seemed to have done them so much good. Soon after the French President resigned in 1969, it was agreed that there should be negotiations on the enlargement of the Community. Satisfactory agreements were made with Britain, Denmark, Norway and Ireland, and as a result, in 1973 The Six became 'The Nine'. In 1972, the Norwegian people had narrowly rejected the agreement in a referendum, and so Norway remained outside the Community.

Britain and European developments, 1945-1973

In June 1940, long before the Coal and Steel Community was launched by the Schuman Declaration, the British Government offered union to France. This initiative marks the crest of a wave of British public support for the federal idea that had swept the country in 1939 and the first half of 1940, to the extent that an Archbishop said[4] it had made a 'staggeringly effective appeal to the British mind' and Churchill was amazed by the enthusiasm with which the Cabinet had approved the offer. The circumstances may have been exceptional, but they did show that the British were capable of embracing the idea of federation. But then the fall of France turned British eyes across the Atlantic; there was a growing disillusion with the continent and an ever-greater reliance on the United States.

In 1945, Britain was the leading European Power, and had been Europe's salvation. It emerged battered but victorious after six years of hostilities. With help from the Empire and American backing, she had thwarted Hitler's ambitions, liberated the continent and proved invincible. It was easy for the British to believe that whilst other less successful nations needed to change, we were all right as we were. There was a growing confidence in the capacity of the British nation-state to do what was necessary for the British people; interest in European union ebbed.

Such notions of superiority were perhaps not too surprising in the circumstances of the time. Britain was proud of its history and traditions. It had not been successfully invaded for nearly nine hundred years, and had developed by evolution rather than revolution. Other European countries had been a prey to internal upheaval, in times past; several had been recently occupied, others defeated. The Channel also served to set us apart, not just geographically but also linguistically, culturally and in our outlook to world affairs; the British were very conscious of the 'foreignness' of those who lived on the Continent.

Britain was very proud of its global role, and its self-image had never been higher. It was a European nation, but this was considered the least important of its 'three circles' in foreign policy; the Empire, which was becoming the Commonwealth, and the United States were the others. A Labour document published in 1950[5] made it clear that in Britain's geo-political agenda, 'in every respect except distance we are closer to our kinsmen in Australia and New Zealand than we are to Europe'. The writer might well have added the USA as well, for under the Labour Government Foreign Secretary Ernest Bevin was committed to Britain's position as a partner of the United States; indeed, Hugo Young describes[6] him as 'Britain's first peace-time Atlanticist'. Neither in 1945, nor for many years after, was Britain willing to commit itself strongly to Europe.

Indeed, in the case of Bevin (and probably many other British people as well) there was some disdain in his attitude to continental countries whose weakness he tended to deride, and in whom he placed 'no hope or reliance'. As Young[7] writes:

Bevin spoke of them with despair, echoing the image sometimes to be found in the Foreign Office documents of the period, which refer to the danger of Britain 'chaining itself to a corpse'. It was one of the things that made him so committed to reawakening Americans' belief that Europe was one of their own most vital national interests.

This detachment from continental affairs surprised and dismayed other European leaders. They tended to assume that having played such a key role in recent events the British would continue to occupy the European stage and act as leading performers in the unfolding drama of their European project. They looked to Britain as a country whose association with freedom and parliamentary government had been amply demonstrated.

1945-the late 1950s

In the early years of closer European cooperation, Britain cheered from the sidelines whilst remaining aloof and detached. We wanted to see a European recovery, and could see the case for greater European unity. It was Churchill who, in his Zurich speech of 1946, spoke of the need 'to build a kind of United States of Europe'. However, Churchill's enthusiasm was for greater European integration in principle, rather than for British participation in practice. Furthermore, he had a definite idea of what Europe was and was not, and in the west the boundary was the English Channel. Most of his plans for continental unification placed England firmly on the outside of such developments, in Young's words[8] acting 'as facilitator, even mere spectator, of the process'. Back in 1930 he had made this clear when he observed:

We have our own dream and our own task. We are with Europe but not of it. We are linked, but not comprised.

Unfortunately, European leaders found his rhetoric compulsive. The phrases were impressive and often seemed so historically significant that it was easy for others to assume he was saying more than he actually meant. By contrast Bevin's oratory was more down-to-earth, but he also had mixed feelings about Europe, at one time seeming sympathetic to what was going on whilst also being concerned to ensure that the plans did not include Britain. For economic reasons, he could see merit in Western Europe achieving a degree of closer economic cooperation. On political grounds, however, he was like Churchill concerned that no power should be ceded to a supranational body. He believed firmly in the nation-state, and would only contemplate cooperation between sovereign governments.

The British were not prepared to go as far as the other European nations, nor at the same speed. This was true of both parties. The **Conservatives** had a pro-European wing, and Churchill put down an unsuccessful motion in the House of Commons calling for the British to participate in the talks leading to the establishment of the Coal and Steel Community. Yet despite his favourable, if vague, expressions of support for the 'European idea', he was too much of a nationalist to wish to see Britain surrender its power to any form of political community involving supranational control. He may have had some doubts as to whether Britain could ever resume its pre-1939 world role. This did not mean he was ready for Britain to settle for a reduced and largely regional one. His fear - widely echoed - was that any such alliance with the continent would reduce the status of the United Kingdom in the world.

The **Labour Party** shared such doubts, and adopted an uncompromisingly negative approach. Prime Minister Attlee knew that participation in the ECSC implied acceptance of a supranational high authority to take key decisions. He thought such an idea 'utterly undemocratic', but was also aware that any pooling of responsibility would lessen the opportunities for socialist planning of the national economy. Therefore, he was not interested in joining the ECSC, though The Six would have liked Britain to do so. His Labour colleague and first Chancellor, Hugh Dalton, elaborated on the British objections:

This approach involves the other partners in the scheme not only in commitments in regard to the coal and steel industries, but also in commitments in regard to the future political framework for Europe. In our view, participation in a political federation, limited to Western Europe, is not compatible either with our Commonwealth ties, our obligations as a member of the wider Atlantic community or as a World Power

Of the British parties, only the **Liberals** were firmly committed to moves for unity in Europe, with Britain working from the inside to influence the outcome of decisions.

With few exceptions, British politicians were suspicious and often dismissive of continental Europe. It was easy to see the six nations of the ECSC as a kind of 'loser's club' in which Britain had no business. Moreover, there was an additional reason for hesitation, one noted[9] by Lynton Robins:
There was...much suspicion of political Catholicism in continental Europe and the major players in the Schuman Plan were known devout Catholics. In this sense, it was easy to see the ECSC as some sort of Catholic plot.

Certainly, the British as a whole never warmed to the Catholic Church, and the Catholic nature of Europe added to anxieties about developments there. The leading pioneers of integration were all of the same religion, and

25
• • •

particularly for some members of the Labour Party this was a problem. Continental Catholics were often hostile to socialism, even when it was largely devoid of any Marxist commitment.

Such misgivings about Britain's place in any forms of European integration were again evident in reactions to the **Pleven Plan** put forward by another Frenchman before the ECSC treaty was even signed. This proposed the pooling of forces from national armies into a common European army, in which German units could be integrated. Britain again gave grudging encouragement, but made it clear that there was no intention to participate. A European Defence Community (EDC), backed by a parallel European Political Community (EPC), would have represented a major step towards European federation. For Europeans, the initiative seemed an obvious and logical development of the functional approach (see opposite), for it was an expansion of cooperation sector by sector. However, in this case the plan proved to be unsuccessful, for an adverse vote in the French National Assembly scuppered the idea.

The prospect of British involvement in an EDC might have encouraged the French to go ahead, but this was never on the cards. Ministers again had doubts about the supranational element involved, especially in such a sensitive and important area as defence and foreign policy. So the British reaction was 'all support short of membership'. The failure of the project was a setback to the dreams of European federalists, to the extent that Duchene has argued[10] that ever since 1954 'political federation as such has never been on the Community agenda. In fact, the federal element in all European integration was cut to the bone'.

British ministers tended to assume that with the failure of the defence proposals the progress towards European cooperation had stalled. In this, they were mistaken. The ECSC was proving a definite success, and the six nations involved move ahead with their plans for a common market. Yet again, when the foreign ministers met in Messina in Italy in 1955 to formulate their plans, the British remained aloof. An under-secretary at the Board of Trade was sent as an observer to report back on the discussions.

When it was obvious that the Messina talks were going to produce something worthwhile, Britain was caught off guard. It was alarmed at the prospect of a trade split between the members of the EEC and any rival free

Theories of postwar integration: a summary

Federalists

They wished to see a rapid movement towards their grand design, complete political unification - as implied by the term a 'United States of Europe'. Their vision and that of the neo-functionalists inspired the post-1945 generation. Spinelli was an enthusiastic federalist.

Functionalists

More cautious in their approach, they preferred to work for unification sector by sector, as seemed necessary and appropriate. They favoured practical cooperation for the more efficient working of different economic and state functions, and would hand over power to a supranational body where this was the best way forward.

Neo-functionalists

They expected integration to come about as a result of 'spillover', which might bring about integration almost by stealth. Intergovernmental meetings can sometimes provide a push towards greater cooperation, via the bargaining process. Monnet could be fitted into this school, for he was always committed to a federal outcome, though he was often vague on detail - hence, the description of him as in an 'incremental federalist'.

Intergovernmentalists

They favoured cooperation between governments for their mutual advantage, a vision rather like de Gaulle's idea of a Europe des Patries. This was an essentially pragmatic rather than a visionary approach.

In postwar Europe, the main arguments over political cooperation have reflected the intergovernmental-supranational debate. Most continentals, be they outright federalists, functionalists or neofunctionalists, have seen the merits of closer union, and for many of them there has been the prospect that this may in time lead to some form of federal outcome. Others, the intergovernmentalists, have been wary of powers being transferred from the national to the Union level, and have sought to slow the pace of change and limit cooperation to the search for mutual benefit.

trade organisation Britain might be instrumental in forming. Because of this it hoped for a wider association of countries which could unite to achieve a customs-free trade in industrial goods, and pressed its case for a Free Trade Area in which there would be no significant surrender of sovereignty, and in which there would be special arrangements for the Commonwealth. For many continentals, this seemed like a deliberate spoiling tactic. They went ahead, and The Six made significant strides in several areas.

In 1960 Britain was instrumental in forming EFTA, the loose free trade association to which we have already referred. It was a more diverse, intergovernmental organisation than the EEC, and lacked distinct political goals. Nonetheless the launch of such a minimalist venture encouraged The Six in their suspicion of British behaviour. De Gaulle and others regarded the initiative as a further example of the British devising a project tailored to their own interests, without much regard to the wishes of others.

A free trade area of the 'outer seven' was much demanded by industrialists in the countries involved. They hoped that an agreement would serve as a platform from which to negotiate with the EEC for a single, integrated European market. Such thinking failed to impress the leading statesmen in the Community.

A change of attitude: 1961 and after

The British approach to European affairs was pragmatic rather than idealistic. It was based firmly upon a perception of British interests, and was not easily swayed by the rhetoric of continental pioneers of unity such as Monnet and Schuman. In his memoirs, Harold Macmillan provided an explanation of the differing mind-sets of the British and the Europeans:
The difference is temperamental and intellectual. It is based on a long divergence of two states of mind and methods of argumentation. The continental tradition likes to reason a priori from the top downwards, from the general principles to the practical application...The Anglo Saxon likes to argue a posteriori from the bottom upwards, from practical experience.

The importance of the Suez Crisis

The Suez Crisis provided a significant shock to many British people. In 1956, the Egyptian President, Colonel Nasser, nationalised the canal which was an important shipping route for this country. British forces intervened, but under threat of economic pressure by the United States the armed action was quickly halted.

Suez shattered many illusions that Britain was still a Great Power. Belief in the American Alliance took a hammering, for the British Government felt exasperated and utterly disillusioned with what ministers saw as American indifference when backing for their deployment of troops was needed. Neither was the Commonwealth a strong ally. It was divided, with only Australia strong in its support; many

Commonwealth countries felt that British policy smacked of imperialism. Given the lack of international approval, British troops were soon withdrawn, and this did not do anything for national morale. To embark on a military adventure of the Suez type and then not carry it through was the worst of all possible policies. The whole episode indicated weakness and relative isolation.

The Cabinet Papers

The 1961 Cabinet Papers contain Prime Minister Macmillan's 37 page memorandum, *The Grand Design*. This was a frank, far-sighted analysis of the decline in British world power. In this and other documents, the reasons for British application to the EC were stated as being primarily political: *The countries of the Common Market, if left to develop alone under French leadership, would grow into a separate political force in Europe...Eventually, it might mean that The Six would come to exercise greater influence than the United Kingdom, both with the United States and possibly with some of the independent countries of the Commonwealth...our interests would be better served by working for a wider European association in which we could play a prominent part.*

The same issues of loss of sovereignty and a federal/confederal future were being discussed by ministers then as they have been more recently, but it was clearly seen that 'we shall become more and more Europeans'. To persuade General de Gaulle to accept British membership of the Common Market, Macmillan was even prepared to share nuclear secrets, and provide France with bombs and technical know-how.

However, seriously practical considerations were to persuade a number of British politicians to amend their outlook to European developments. For several years, Britain had been slow to adjust to a decline in world status, and only in the late 1950s did attitudes begin to change. In world terms, the enforced withdrawal from Suez in 1956 (see opposite), the loosening of Commonwealth ties as countries achieved independence and increasing doubts about the 'special relationship' with the United States, highlighted a loss of British power and influence. At home, there were balance of payments difficulties and a lack-lustre 'stop-go' economy, whilst on the continent The Six benefited from their expanded market.

As the new decade loomed on the horizon, many of the reasons for scepticism about the EEC seemed less important. The early success of the EEC helped to promote new thinking in London, for ministers could see obvious advantages in sharing in the industrial development of Europe, with its large market of over 180m people and its impressive rate of economic growth. With Britain inside the Community, there would be a vast population of some 240m, comparable to that of the USSR and larger than the United States. In such an arena, Britain would have a greater say in world affairs, and deal with the USA more as a partner than as an increasingly poor relation.

The first British application to join the EEC, 1961

In July 1961, the Macmillan Government announced that Britain would pursue an application for membership of the EEC. This was a major departure in policy, signifying a change of direction in Britain's external relations. Handled in a deliberately low key manner, the initiative was presented as purely a trading matter, without political complications. There was no attempt to persuade the electorate of the merits of the European Idea. Indeed, the Prime Minister's rhetoric still included references to the country's important world role and its key relationship with the United States.

In October 1961, negotiations got underway, with Edward Heath (the Lord Privy Seal) leading the British team. In January 1963, General de Gaulle vetoed this application (see opposite). He was a strong nationalist who wanted the Community to have a powerful voice, preferably one with a French accent. He claimed that Britain was not yet ready to be admitted. She was distracted by her Commonwealth interests, and was too much of an Atlantic power to be truly committed to a European destiny. He explained his position in a speech in Paris, in the month of his rejection:

It must be agreed that the entry first of Great Britain, and of (other) states, will completely change the series of adjustments, agreements, compensations and regulations already established between the Six. We would then have to envisage the construction of another Common Market which ... would without any doubt no longer resemble the one the Six have built ... in the end, there would be a colossal Atlantic Community under American domination.

Certainly, there were many 'reluctant Europeans' in Britain for whom the driving-force of our application was a fear of being left behind in a highly competitive economic race. There was little sign of a desire to think in genuine European terms.

The second application, 1969

In 1967, under the Wilson (Labour) Government, Britain tried again, along with Denmark, Norway and the Irish Republic. The Government was attracted by the potential of a large single market, and believed that joint research and shared development-costs in high technology industries would prove beneficial to British manufacturers. It was suggested that British entry would give the Community a new dynamism, and that Britain's capacity for technological innovation would be an asset.

The failure of Britain's first bid

When de Gaulle exercised his veto in January 1963 and the attempt to join the Common Market failed, it was easy to blame the French leader. The imperious way in which he ended the bid ensured that general and informed opinion was critical, and contemporary opinion polls showed that only 17% of those questioned held the British Government culpable for the setback. Macmillan has been absolved of any serious criticism in most assessments. Some more recent studies have dissented from this view, and a German one has actually suggested that Macmillan knew that de Gaulle would block British entry even before the formal application was made. Others have criticised his personal diplomacy with de Gaulle and Adenauer, in particular the failure to persuade them or offer any incentives in order to obtain their support.

In particular, in an interesting paper **Piers Ludlow** has detected[11] three flaws in the British approach:

- **The conditional nature of the bid**, which was concerned to find out the terms on which entry might be possible. As the negotiations continued, more and more requests for concessions for the Commonwealth, EFTA and the British farmers were made.
- **Domestic Reticence**, the reluctance of ministers to confront critics of their new policy head-on, and to sell the decision to join. The Prime Minister was too gentle with the Euro-sceptics of his day, for they were all people with a substantial following and power-base within the party. In August 1961 the Economist was moved to observe that the application was covered in a `bower of ifs and buts`.
- **Flawed bilateral diplomacy**. Macmillan believed that skilful handling of the European leaders in bilateral discussions would overcome any difficulties. However, at the time Chancellor Adenauer of Germany saw France as a more useful partner, finding particular comfort in de Gaulle`s strong backing for German interests in Berlin at the time when

the Cold War was still a key fact of European life. De Gaulle had serious reservations, and did not believe that Europe would be strengthened by British participation. He felt that Britain was too close to the United States, and feared that with Britain inside the Community America would have too much influence in its affairs. France's dominance among The Six would be imperilled. De Gaulle also claimed that the Commonwealth would be a drain on Community resources, and that Britain was not as yet ready to be a 'good European'.

Whatever the real reasons for failure, publicly blame was heaped on de Gaulle's shoulders and Britain's own hesitations and miscalculations were all but forgotten. This made Edward Heath's task in 1971-72 easier than otherwise might have been the case. If Britain's first bid had ended in a technical impasse, or - much worse - a Parliamentary rejection of the terms, renewed negotiations would have been more difficult.

The attempt was nonetheless again frustrated by de Gaulle, though - as previously - the application was not withdrawn. This time the French veto came before negotiations even began. No longer could Britain be said to be more concerned about Commonwealth interests, and other members wanted Britain to join. Rather, he argued that Britain was still too subservient to the USA, and that her ailing economy would be a drag on the rest of the Community.

Britain had moved some considerable way from its earlier post-war stance of detachment from Europe. Even ministers in the Labour Government tended to see the EEC less as a threat and more as a means of national salvation, although there was little enthusiasm within the party for European entanglements.

The third application, 1970

De Gaulle resigned in 1969 (and died a year later), and this boosted Britain's chances of successful negotiations. By now, the pro-European Edward Heath (see also p137 for a discussion on his case for entry) was Prime Minister, and the French President, Georges Pompidou, was personally and politically sympathetic to him. Pompidou did not have any rooted objection to British membership. Moreover, fears of growing German power and independence were developing in France, and he understood that Britain might prove to be a useful counterweight within the Community.

This change of disposition across the Channel eased what were sometimes difficult discussions. The new warmth helped to bring this third attempt to a successful conclusion, and Heath was determined to overcome any remaining obstacles. In October 1971, the House of Commons accepted the principle of entry into the EEC, and thereby accession to the Rome treaties. The Treaty of Accession was signed in January 1972, and Britain joined a year later, along with Denmark and Ireland.

Those politicians who argued for entry largely confined themselves to generalisations on the political issues involved. They were keen to reassure people that sovereignty was not an issue. In many speeches, the economic case for entry was expounded, namely access to a larger market and the allegedly beneficial effects of a blast of European competition on British industry. Comments were sometimes made about the beneficial effects of the Community in setting aside the historic Franco-German rivalries, the value of greater unity and cooperation in Europe, and the opportunity for Britain to retain a voice in European discussions of great questions of the day. Sovereignty was dismissed as being a distracting question of no particular relevance, but it was to return a couple of decades later to haunt policy-makers.

CONCLUSION

For many years British statesmen were taken aback by the single-mindedness with which the Europeans pursued their integrationist goals. They assumed that proposals would not materialise or, if they did materialise, would not work. They also disliked the direction of many of these initiatives, which tended to emphasise supranational or federal goals even if the means to reach the ultimate destination were functionalist in approach. The British, whilst broadly approving of plans for greater unity on the continent, envisaged a looser form of unity. They favoured inter-governmental solutions to particular problems, believing that participation in any form of political federation was incompatible with our global responsibilities.

By the early 1960s, the British attitude to developments on the continent was being re-assessed. In a Europe of 'sixes' and 'sevens', Britain was in the outer, less influential tier. Against a background of EEC success and diminishing British influence, many politicians perceived - or came to be convinced - that our future was to be increasingly based on the European circle, even if the Commonwealth and Atlantic ties remained strong. With such considerations in mind, Britain finally entered the EEC. A new era in Britain's external relations was about to begin.

Britain and the European Community: from entry to Maastricht

INTRODUCTION

Within the EEC there had long been discussion over the merits of widening as opposed to deepening the Community. Fears had been expressed by the French in particular that British participation would be associated with a loosening of the ties between member states, and the experience of the decade or so after the first enlargement seemed to lend some support to these anxieties. Some steps were taken to strengthen the links, in particular the formation of the European Monetary System (EMS) and the move to direct elections for the European Parliament. However, on the whole, the period was one of stagnation rather than development.

The initiatives surrounding the single market, the single currency and the social charter gave a new impetus to the Community from the mid-1980s, and the leadership provided by Jacques Delors as President of the European Commission was instrumental in taking the EC further down the road of closer cooperation. This process reached its high water-mark at Maastricht in 1991. Thereafter, there were positive moves on the one hand, but growing doubts about the merits of ever-stronger ties on the other.

ASK YOURSELF

- Why did progress towards cooperation within the Community stall in the decade and a half after Britain signed the Treaty of Accession?
- Why did the Conservatives show less enthusiasm and commitment to Europe after 1979?
- Why was Britain keen on the creation of a single market but un-enthusiastic about the creation of a single currency (see also p121-125)?
- How did the Labour approach to Europe evolve in the years after 1979?
- In what ways was Margaret Thatcher anti-European?

MAIN TEXT

The years up until the early 1970s were good ones for The Six. Europe was peaceful, business was thriving. After that, things became more problematic. The widening of membership coincided with the energy crisis, and a developing recession in the western world. In October 1973, the Oil and Petroleum Exporting Countries (OPEC) quadrupled the price of crude oil, and the EC, which imported 63% of its energy requirements, was badly hit. In its reaction to the crisis, the Community was torn by schism, and the 1970s also saw a number of other internal disagreements.

Against this background of recession, states were inevitably more interested in protectionism than integrationism. Their economies diverged significantly, and for Britain and Italy especially there was much concern about the level of inflation. In both countries, the fear was that closer integration might be associated with policies of deflation and a consequent growth in unemployment.

The behaviour of new members - in particular, Britain - was seen as a contributory factor in this era of '**Euro-sclerosis**'. In the 1970s and 1980s, Britain and to a lesser extent Denmark tended to resist any proposals which might endanger national sovereignty and promote closer bonds. However, even if Britain did little to help lift the Community from its malaise, it was not the only member state responsible for the years of negativism and unease.

Further expansion of the Community

In 1981, Greece entered the EC, and thus made it a Community of 'The Ten'. Spain and Portugal joined in 1986, so that there were by then twelve members. (It is here appropriate to add that in 1994 Austria, Finland and Sweden were added to The Twelve. In 2000, therefore, fifteen nations are currently members). Greenland (a Danish territory) voted to leave the Community in a referendum held in 1982; it officially left in January 1985. Greenlanders were unhappy about the application of EC fisheries policy and felt remote from the distant 'Brussels bureaucracy'. Following the unification of Germany in 1990, the area and population of the Community was boosted by the accession of the Eastern sector.

Britain's position in the European Community

Before the 1970 election, Harold Wilson had begun to prepare the ground for a possible change of tack should the Conservatives be victorious at the polls. Whilst in the House of Commons he appeared to remain committed to another British bid for membership, but when speaking to party members in the country he was more scathing about the terms the Tories would be prepared to accept. The Labour Party at large was never enthusiastic about membership, and once in opposition the leader dropped the bipartisanship and sounded more hostile to entry unless the terms were very favourable. Such a seeming reversal of policy was the price paid for holding the party together on a highly divisive issue.

The Labour leadership did not approve of the terms of entry obtained by the Heath Government (1970-1974) and whilst in Opposition it decided that the question of Britain's membership would be submitted to the electorate as soon as Labour returned to power. Some renegotiation occurred after 1974, although many commentators have argued that the changes were little more than what would be expected from the routine matter of day-to-day compromise in policy negotiation. However, the new Government then felt justified in commending the revised terms to the British people in a referendum campaign. As the Prime Minister[1] told the House of Commons: *My judgement is that on an assessment of all which has been achieved and all that has changed, to remain in the Community is best for Britain, for Europe, for the Commonwealth, for the third world and the wider world.*

The question asked of the voters was straightforward:
Do you think that the United Kingdom should stay in the European Community (The Common Market)?

In June 1975, Britain voted by 17,378,581 to 8,470,073 in favour of 'staying in', a 67.5% 'yes' vote on a 63.2% turnout.

The Conservatives and Europe, after 1979

Over the following years, the British had the reputation in Europe of being half-hearted about membership. On a series of issues, British representatives defended the Government's position forcefully, and the tone of this defence sharpened noticeably after Margaret Thatcher's victory in 1979. She was committed to reductions in public expenditure, and the

37

pursuit of this goal led her into dispute over aspects of EC policy. Two
areas of particular contention in the early years concerned:
i. the expense and effectiveness of the Common Agricultural Policy (see also
    p118-123)
ii. Britain's budgetary contribution to the EC.

The issues were linked. Britain's objection, firmly advocated by the Prime
Minister, was that overall the country was paying vastly more into the
Community than it got back out of it. In respect of the years 1980-1982, the
excess amounted to £1,014m. At that time, nearly three-quarters of the EC
budget was being used to support agriculture. Great Britain did not much
benefit from this, for we had the lowest workforce engaged in farming on the
continent (less than 3%). On the other hand, help in the ailing regions and
the modernisation of traditional industries were of more concern to Britain.
Compared to 74% of the 1978 budget being spent on farming, only 4% was
spent on the Regional Fund the purpose of which was to make grants to
places suffering from low income, chronic unemployment or declining
population such as Central Scotland.

The Prime Minister was not one to readily compromise, and she was
unimpressed by the rhetorical flourishes of her colleagues at the negotiating
table. She wanted 'our money' back, and was prepared to insist at whatever
cost to relations with the other member countries. Britain had a case about
the imbalance of its budgetary contributions, but it was pursued in a way
which antagonised the leaders of France and Germany, and other heads of
government. As one of them remarked, it was like being hit with a handbag!

Roy Jenkins, then the President of the European Commission, has given[2] us
an amusing account of Mrs Thatcher's attitude at his first meeting of the
European Council:
*Towards the end, Mrs Thatcher got the discussions bogged down by being too
demanding. Her mistake...arose out of her having only one of the three
qualities of a great advocate. She has nerve and determination to win, but
she does not have a good understanding of the case against her...her
reiterated cry of `It's my money. I want it back` strikes an insistently jarring
note. She lacks the third quality...of not boring the judge and jury...She only
understood four out of the fourteen or so points on the British side and
repeated each of them twenty-seven times during the evening.*

The dispute between Britain and the rest of the Community was finally resolved in 1984 at Fontainebleau, when President Mitterrand was helpful in producing a compromise formula by which Britain had a rebate of 66% of the difference between its VAT contributions and what it obtained back in benefits.

The Thatcher approach

Like other Prime Ministers with the exception of Edward Heath, Margaret Thatcher seemed to be logically convinced of the merits of membership of the Community, but not emotionally committed. She made a cool appraisal of Britain's position, and was sure that Britain needed to 'stay in' for sound commercial reasons.

She certainly did not share the vision of the creators of post-war Europe, and was out of sympathy with plans for political union between The Twelve. Early pioneers dreamed of Churchill's 'United States of Europe' as a desirable long-term objective. A number of statesmen since then, such as Willi Brandt of (what was then) West Germany and later Mitterrand, saw practical benefits in ever-closer cooperation. Whilst such politicians liked the idea of moving towards some kind of federal Europe, the British Government took an entirely different stance, more reminiscent of the Gaullist approach. The General spoke, as she did and still does, of a 'Europe des Patries', a Europe of member states which work together for mutual convenience and national self-interest. She dismissed thoughts of closer union as impractical, unnecessary and undesirable.

Her thinking on Europe was an amalgam of economic liberalism and nationalistic conservatism. The economic liberal in her could find good reasons for signing the **Single European Act (SEA)** of 1986, which committed Britain to the creation in 1992 of a single European market, an 'area without frontiers', in which the 'free movement of goods, persons, services and capital' was ensured. The original concept of the Community was that it should be a 'Common Market', a free-trade area without any restraints to trade, but some regulations and barriers had never been eliminated and others developed in the enlarged Community. The idea of the new development was acceptable to British ministers who favoured open trading conditions, and had since 1979 allowed the free movement of currency into and out of Britain.

39

The nationalist in Margaret Thatcher was to make her uneasy about the consequences of the very measure to which she had agreed. In signing the SEA, The Twelve committed themselves to movement towards monetary union, a goal to be 'progressively realised'. The phrase is to be found in the Preamble, rather than in the main legally-binding clauses of the Act. At the time, she seemed to be unaware of such detail, as she did of another statement in the same section which spoke of the Act as marking another step towards 'ever-closer-union' of the European peoples. In her memoirs, she subsequently wrote[3] that she had 'surrendered no significant British interest' in agreeing to the SEA. Yet the Act did indeed represent a significant move towards integration among the member states.

As part of the main text, there was a commitment to lessen disparities between the richer and poorer areas of the Community, known as the policy of 'cohesion'. Accordingly, more resources were to be allocated to the 'structural funds', for regional and social expenditure. Provision was also made for closer cooperation in the area of foreign policy and security, and for environmental improvement. All national legislatures ratified the Act in 1987, including the Westminster Parliament. There was an initial threat of a rebellion in the House of Lords for, as in other countries, there was some unease over the loss of sovereignty involved. Because of these constitutional implications, Denmark and Ireland held referendums prior to ratification.

Economic and monetary union

A Report was drawn up by the President of the European Commission, Jacques Delors, and presented to the Council of Ministers in June 1989. He was a committed federalist, and his name was to become synonymous with that of the EC over the coming years. His programme envisaged a three-stage progression to the ultimate goal of full monetary union:

Stage One involved the removal of all barriers to a free market, as laid down in the 1986 Act, with all countries participating in the European Monetary System (see opposite).
Stage Two involved the creation of a Central European Bank, to co-ordinate the national banks of member countries (e.g., the German Bundesbank and the Bank of England).
Stage Three involved a fixed exchange-rate between the European currencies, to be achieved by the use of a single currency, the Ecu (now known as the Euro). The Italian 'lira' and British 'pound' would disappear.

When these stages were completed, there would be full monetary union with important fiscal and monetary decisions being taken at the European level. The Bank would be able to impose constraints on national budgets.

Many of the European currencies were already linked in the **European Monetary System**, devised in 1979. One of the most well-known elements of the European Monetary System was the **Exchange Rate Mechanism (ERM)**. This was a system of fixed exchange rates, with each currency allowed to fluctuate by only 2.25% from its stated value to other currencies.

Britain did not join the EMS when it was founded, but in 1989-1990, there was pressure on ministers to enter the Exchange Rate Mechanism. Those in favour of British membership included many voices in industry, the City and at Westminster. Labour, the party formerly so cool on Europe, had also come out in favour, and the more pro-Europeans in the Cabinet saw membership as the inevitable and desirable next step.

Supporters of British membership felt that it would provide greater stability for the pound, and that in the future there would be no need to have high interest rates to 'prop it up' when it was under pressure. There would be less temptation for currency speculators to buy or sell sterling if it was not subject to fluctuations in value; it would also make it easier for businessmen to plan ahead if they knew that the value of the exchange rate would not fluctuate so wildly. They also believed that it would help in the battle against inflation, for membership would impose a straight-jacket on the British economy and force governments to adopt policies of fiscal rectitude. Opponents lamented precisely this constraint. They felt that Britain would lose much of its freedom of manoeuvre by a surrender of its economic sovereignty.

Margaret Thatcher's gut instincts were against any attempts to link sterling to other currencies in this way and thereby 'buck the market'. She laid down stringent conditions which would need to be met before Britain could join, but kept up a kind of unity in the Cabinet by opting for the formula that Britain would join 'when the time was right'. Many suspected that it would never be so for her, but eventually the Foreign Secretary and Chancellor were influential in bringing about British entry in October 1990.

A number of commentators believe that Britain joined at an inopportune moment when sterling was at too high a level. At the time of entry, it stood at 2.95 deutschmarks, and it was allowed to vary between 2.78 and 3.13. At such a level, membership helped keep imports and inflation down, but made the task of exporters difficult because British goods were made relatively dear in other countries. Some people wanted a realignment of currency values within the ERM, whilst others thought that to demonstrate confidence in the pound and in British membership we should seek an early opportunity to join a narrower band.

A social charter

The Single Market was concerned with the elimination of trade barriers between countries so that there would be a free market in goods and labour. To Delors, the EC was more than a common market, it was 'an organised space governed by commonly agreed rules that (would) ensure economic and social cohesion, and equality of opportunity'. In other words, there was a social dimension to the market, which involved the protection of individual rights so that the Community worked for the benefit of all its citizens.

In May 1989, the EC produced a draft *Charter of Fundamental Social Rights* in connection with terms of employment. It was a bold document, but largely as a result of pressure from the British Government it was much watered-down in its next version. The rights secured were more limited in scope, so that proposals concerning a minimum wage, pensions for the elderly and worker-participation in company decision-making were dropped, and other items diluted. Even the revised form was unacceptable to British ministers who alone refused to go along with the proposals.

Margaret Thatcher was wary of any idea advanced by Delors who she described in her memoirs[4] as 'a fully-fledged spokesman for federalism'. In her view, he was damned as a Frenchman, a Catholic and a socialist. She was totally opposed to a document which threatened to reintroduce by the back door those elements of socialism which she had thrown out of the front one over the previous decade. She saw it as a 'socialist charter', a piece of discredited social engineering which smacked of 'the era of Karl Marx and the class struggle'. It was precisely because it offered the chance to re-establish social rights involving conditions of employment that the Labour movement in Britain liked it so much. Indeed, it was largely the visit of 'Frere Jacques' to the TUC Conference in 1989, and his assurances about the social dimension, that had helped to wean the movement away from its previous anti-Europeanism (see also p95-96).

The period between the passing of the SEA and the signing of the Maastricht Treaty was to be one in which the Commission became a particularly powerful force within the Community. Under Delors' assertive leadership, it had a central role in paving the way for the single market. However, the driving force was the European Council. It took the decision to summon the two IGCs whose work was preparatory to the signing of the 1991 document.

The approach to Maastricht, 1991

In the months leading to the Maastricht summit, issues such as the Social Charter, the single currency and the 'democratic deficit' (see p73-77) were much argued over by politicians and in the press. There was due to be a settlement of a number of European issues, with a view to signing a treaty which would set out the target dates for achieving the next stages of the Delors Plan. Many Conservatives - Margaret Thatcher among them - expressed strong hostility to the author of these suggestions, for they realised that he wished to see a massive transfer of power to Brussels and away from individual governments. His comment back in 1988 that he expected to see 80% of all legislation in member-countries coming from Brussels within ten years had convinced many of his critics that the implications of any proposals from him needed to be carefully studied.

Labour was keen to keep a step ahead of the Government by showing a cautious willingness to embrace each new stage. The Conservatives in the late Autumn of 1991 were in turmoil. Critics of closer union felt that Britain had gone far enough; the single market of 1992 was fine, but other proposals were not to their liking. Some of them failed to appreciate that the Preamble to the Single European Act had committed the country to further progress towards unity.

It was left to the Maastricht Summit to resolve the conflicting opinions between the member-states. The Dutch decision to meet in its oldest city was a sign of true 'Europeanism' for - as its city fathers proudly proclaimed - it was European long before it was Dutch. It had a long and bloody history of conflict and was fought over by many European rulers. But, sandwiched between Germany and Belgium, it stayed loyal to the Netherlands of which it remained a part.

43

Margaret Thatcher: her approach to Europe assessed

Margaret Thatcher's approach to matters European was in some respects in line with the attitudes expressed by some of her predecessors. Admittedly her rhetoric and style were distinctive, so that she seemed markedly more hostile than many of those around her. Yet faced with thorny issues, her instinct was to assert traditional British interests and to be wary of any schemes which smacked of supranationalism. Arguably, she was unlucky that the later period of her premiership happened to coincide with another in a series of periodic spurts of enthusiasm within the EC which pushed Europe further towards integration. She was therefore the person whose task she believed it was to resist the integrationist tide.

In the same way that Attlee had turned down the chance of British involvement in the ECSC, so she found the idea of a single currency unacceptable. A common currency she could accept, for this might exist alongside national currencies. But a single one was a step too far, associated as it was with moves towards closer integration. She preferred the policy of countries uniting in a trading organisation, in the same way that in the late fifties British ministers had shown interest in creating a free trade area as an alternative to the EEC.

Her approach was pragmatic, whereas that of the Europeans was idealistic. For her, the idea of a common currency was a practical and attainable one, in the British tradition. But it was not what most of her fellow European leaders wanted, for it was not rooted in the federal ideas to which many of them subscribed. The goal of unity in Europe was an adventurous journey on which they were happy to embark. She had no interest in the so-called European Idea, and was unimpressed by talk of federalism or any 'United States of Europe'.

Her outlook was clearly expressed in her **Bruges Speech** of 1988. Having reviewed the British contribution to Europe over the centuries and denounced the idea of a 'European superstate', she pointed out that - contrary to its pretensions - the EC 'was not the only manifestation of European identity...We shall always look on Warsaw, Prague and Budapest as great European cities'. She went on to express her own preferences:

Willing and active co-operation between independent sovereign states is the best way to build a successful European Community... Europe will be stronger precisely because it has France as France, Spain as Spain, Britain as Britain, each with its own customs, traditions and identity. It would be folly to try to fit them into some sort of identikit European personality.

She ended on a high note, which she would see as far from anti-European:

Let Europe be a family of nations, understanding each other better, appreciating each other more, doing more together, but relishing our national identity no less than our common European endeavour. Let us have a Europe which plays its full part in the wider world, which looks outward not inward, and which preserves that Atlantic Community - that Europe on both sides of the Atlantic - which is our noblest inheritance and our greatest strength.

If she lacked enthusiasm for the hopes which inspired some fellow European leaders, she was not a Little Englander. She was interested in widening the European Community so that the countries of Central and Eastern Europe might be brought into its orbit, for as she remarked[5] on another occasion; 'Europe is older than the European Community. I want the larger, wider Europe in which Moscow is also a European Power'. In her memoirs, she makes it clear that a supranational EC had little to offer to meet the 'aspirations and needs' of 'those millions of Eastern Europeans [then] living under communism'.

Ultimately her vision was of an EC which was open to all, and which preserved 'the diversity and nationhood of each of its members'. In the words of Lynton Robins[6]:

What Mrs Thatcher was seeking, like three out of her four predecessors, was a looser, outward-looking partnership of European nations, which was not opposed to Atlanticist ties, and which was intergovernmental in character rather than based on the proto-federalist institutions of the Community.

Such a vision was not markedly dissimilar to that of Wilson and Callaghan before her, even if the tone in which it was expressed was considerably more shrill. Her distaste for European union was in line with theirs', but in her case it was thrown into negative relief when matched against the idealistic

statements from the continent.

Europe was to prove the issue which wrecked Mrs Thatcher's premiership. It caused directly or indirectly the loss of key ministers in her Government, notably Michael Heseltine, Leon Brittan, Nigel Lawson, Nicholas Ridley and Sir Geoffrey Howe. Of all the casualties, however, the main one was the Prime Minister herself. Howe's resignation speech was devastating, for he ridiculed her view of 'a continent that is positively teeming with ill-intentioned people, scheming, in her words, to extinguish democracy, to "dissolve our national identities", to lead us "through the back door into a federal Europe"'. The resignation triggered the leadership challenge which brought about her downfall in November 1990.

CONCLUSION

The resignation of Margaret Thatcher at first seemed to represent the end of an era in which her 'uniquely bleak vision of Europe'[7] had held sway. Her premiership coincided with much of the early period of British membership of the EC, and - like her two immediate predecessors - she was no instinctive

45

• • •

European, if the term was conceived as implying support for the European Community.

Her removal indicated a rift within the governing elite over the British approach to Europe. Those deemed as pro-Europeans were not wild proponents of full European integration. Rather they were people worried by the dangers they perceived if Britain lagged behind the other member states, at a time when they were bent on moving forwards. For them, there was no alternative for Britain to membership, and they wanted to see an administration prepared to make it work.

From Maastricht to Amsterdam

INTRODUCTION

The passage of the Single European Act had brought about a new dynamism within the European community. There was pressure for progress in other spheres, and many of the issues were up for discussion at Maastricht in late 1991. Maastricht represented an attempt to provide a blueprint for integration, but the treaty was devised against a background of much uncertainty about the future state of Europe. Dramatic changes were taking place in Central and Eastern Europe: the end of the Cold War, the reunification of Germany and the breakdown of Soviet rule in the satellite states as well as in the USSR itself. Such developments raised new issues about economic prosperity and democratic stability on the continent, and made it necessary for British policy-makers to think again about their ideas of Europe.

In the period since the Maastricht summit, divisions over Europe have been seriously exposed. The weakness of Britain's position within the European Union has become ever-more-apparent. On occasions, we have been able to slow down the progress towards integration, but not to halt the momentum in the direction of closer union.

The election of a new Labour government in 1997 opened up the possibility of a more positive approach to matters European. The early steps taken by the Blair Administration suggested that this more pro-European stance could be part of a wider strategy of modernising the body politic.

47

ASK YOURSELF

- What were the main issues in need of resolution at Maastricht?
- In what respects did the signing of the Maastricht Treaty represent a turning-point in European affairs?
- To what extent, post-Maastricht, are we living in a new intergovernmental phase of EU activity?
- Why did the Major Government find European issues so difficult to handle?
- Is Britain under New Labour still a 'reluctant European'?

MAIN TEXT

The issue of Europe had helped to bring about Margaret Thatcher's downfall, and in retirement she was to gun for the Maastricht Treaty and generally make life harder for her successor by exposing the disunity within the party over European policy. **John Major** soon made it clear that he wished to place Britain 'at the heart of Europe', and he played a leading role in the negotiations at Maastricht.

The Treaty of Maastricht, December 1991

The Treaty on European Union was negotiated and signed at Maastricht. In the words of the Preamble, it was designed to achieve 'an ever closer union among the peoples of Europe where decisions are taken as closely as possible to the citizens'. It created a European Union, which had four objectives:
- The promotion of economic and social progress, particularly via economic and monetary union
- The implementation of a foreign and security policy
- Cooperation in the areas of justice and home affairs
- The establishment of joint citizenship.

As the pace of integration was scheduled to vary in each case, it was decided to base the Union on three separate sections or 'pillars', each of which would have its own institutional structure. These pillars were:

i. The new European Community

This was a development of what was already been happening. It covered economic and monetary union, and added new policies to those already falling within the scope of the Treaty of Rome. In many ways, it formalised the Community's commitment to what was then current practice. Maastricht took the SEA a stage further. Internal frontiers were already due to be abolished by January 1993, and the new Treaty decreed that citizens of member-states automatically became members of the **European Union**. As such, they could live and work in any member state, stand for municipal office or for the European Parliament wherever they live, and vote in the country of residence.

The **key clauses** were those concerned with the irrevocable path to economic and monetary union (EMU). For member countries to be permitted to join EMU, they must attain a certain standard of economic performance, by meeting the 'convergence' criteria (see p126). There were also institutional changes. The Parliament acquired greater powers, particularly over the appointment of the Commission. It was to be responsible for the appointment of an Ombudsman who would look into instances of maladministration by EU institutions.

ii. & iii. The other two pillars

The other two pillars were based on intergovernmental cooperation outside the scope of the existing treaties, though provision was made for reporting on them to the Council and Parliament. The second concerned foreign policy and defence, and was intended 'to assert the Community's identity on the international scene'. It covered all aspects of European security, and included provisions for the eventual framing of a common defence policy, backed by a common defence force. Decision-making was generally to be exercised through unanimity, though the governments could decide to take implementing decisions by majority voting. The third was concerned with policing, asylum and immigration control. The intention was to agree a common asylum policy by the beginning of 1993, and to develop police cooperation to combat drug-trafficking and organised crime, through EUROPOL, the new international police unit.

....

In addition to the main treaty, there were 17 Protocols and 33 Declarations. The most important Protocol was that on Social Policy, which was designed to improve working conditions and industrial employment practices. This provision (previously known as the Social Charter) is now better known as the **Social Chapter** (see p127-129).

Initially, the agreements reached and obligations accepted at Maastricht were hailed as a significant breakthrough. The problems associated with ratification were soon to mar this impression. Moreover, the compromises involved had been achieved at a cost. Britain, as we shall see, opted out of two key aspects of the Maastricht process. Previously, membership had implied acceptance of 'acquis communautaire' - the sum of all past EC treaties and policies - in full, plus an agreement that there should be unanimity on all matters of future Community development. The British opt-outs, and the Danish ones which followed, broke new ground. In so doing, they created the prospect of a Europe which moves forward at different speeds on different issues, with some countries in the fast lane and others bringing up the rear (see also p166-167).

Britain and the Maastricht Treaty

The British drew back from two major provisions. By a special Protocol, the Government declined to commit itself to involvement in economic and monetary union, whilst reserving the right to join in either when it got underway or at a later date. Also, it refused to 'sign up' for the Social Chapter, though Britain could specifically 'opt in' to any of its provisions. On John Major's return, the Maastricht settlement was presented as a negotiating triumph, and it was claimed that Britain had won 'game, set and match'. With an election looming, this was a useful boost to his reputation as a statesman.

Difficulties over ratification

The Prime Minister's problems were to follow after the 1992 election. For the Maastricht Treaty to come into force, it had to be ratified by all the parliaments of all the member-states. The process of ratification soon ran into difficulties, though the Treaty was approved by the European Parliament early in 1992. In a referendum in June 1992, the Danish people narrowly decided that they did not want to accept the Treaty. For the Treaty to go ahead after this rejection, the Danes needed to be taken on board, and this involved a second referendum. The Community was unwilling to allow any renegotiation of the actual Treaty, but further elaboration of some points and clarification of others, was inevitable.

In June, the Irish voted strongly in favour of the Treaty, but in September, the French gave it only the narrowest endorsement. The British Government decided not to have a referendum, and ministers pledged to go ahead with ratification despite the signs of mounting opposition in Europe. The Maastricht Bill was brought before the House of Commons and given a Second Reading in May, 1992. The Prime Minister sold it to his right-wing as an anti-centralising Treaty, emphasising what the Government had not signed up for. Labour broadly accepted the economic, social and political framework of the Treaty, but could not endorse the Government's position because of its double 'opt-out'. It particularly disliked the decision not to embrace the Social Chapter.

By the end of the year, the Third Reading was slowly proceeding, and at the Edinburgh Council meeting several loose ends were tied up. Measures were taken to resolve the Danish problem, and there was agreement on the details of new budgetary arrangements. However, the main aspect which pleased the British Prime Minister was that flesh was put on the bones of the idea of **subsidiarity** (see overleaf), a concept which had been written into the Maastricht Treaty. This helped him to claim that the Treaty was a decentralising measure, the more so as it was agreed that the European Commission was to withdraw laws in some limited areas.

In reality, it is difficult to see that the new emphasis on subsidiarity changed very much. The implication of the doctrine was that national policies would in future be the norm, but countries more committed to greater integration were always likely to press their case strongly. In any legal dispute which ensued, the integrationist Court of Justice was likely to veer towards a 'European' solution.

What really damaged John Major's position over Europe was the situation in the money markets in September 1992. Following entry into the ERM, all had seemed to go well; the pound's value was maintained and interest rates gradually fell. However by mid-1992 there were developing strains in the system, and the pound began to slide. Dealers were becoming increasingly concerned about the depth of the British recession and the still too-high interest rates which were holding back any chance of recovery. Sterling was under threat, and the pound sank to the bottom of the ERM band as dealers anticipated a possible devaluation. The sense of uncertainty was worsened by the prospect of a very close French referendum result. On **Crisis Day**,

Subsidiarity

The doctrine of 'subsidiarity' was first put forward by Pope Pius XI in 1931; for him, it meant **'government at the lowest possible level'**. It was resurrected in the late 1980s, and it means that the Union should only undertake those tasks which states cannot perform for themselves. In late 1992, the British Government placed much emphasis on the idea, for it seemed to be useful ammunition against those Tory right-wingers who feared that a 'federal super-state' was being created on the foundations of Maastricht. Subsidiarity could help to tame the so-called 'Brussels Monster', and bring about a decentralisation of decision-making.

Subsidiarity was written into the Maastricht Treaty, which insisted that decisions should be taken 'as closely as possible to the citizen'. In Article 3b, it was spelt out that:

In areas which do not fall within its exclusive competence, the Community shall take action, in accordance with the principle of subsidiarity, only if and in so far as the objectives for the proposed action cannot be sufficiently achieved by the Member States and can therefore, by reason of the scale or effects of the proposed action, be better achieved by the Community. Any action by the Community shall not go beyond what is necessary to achieve the objectives of this Treaty.

Jacques Delors tried to reassure the British and others, by stressing that under the principle, matters such as internal security, justice, planning, education, culture and health should remain the responsibility of member states. Some continental MEPs expressed the concern that subsidiarity could be used as an excuse to weaken European integration. They feared that the cloak of subsidiarity was being used to enable the British Government to 'kill off' environmental and social directives in which Britain lagged behind.

At the Edinburgh Council, new procedures were agreed to 'fill out' the doctrine which only has much meaning when applied to particular policies. In future, national power was to be the rule, and EC power the exception. The EC was to act only when member states could not achieve the desired goal as well themselves. There was no question of challenging its existing powers. However, the Commission has subsequently agreed to withdraw or amend 21 pieces of actual and draft legislation, as opposed to the 72 favoured by Britain. They included matters such as the treatment of animals in zoos, the harmonisation of gambling regulations and certain food labelling directives.

September 16, the Bank of England desperately tried to prop up sterling, but despite resorting to very high interest rates, it was unable to defend the pound from speculators. In these circumstances, the pound was withdrawn from the ERM, and allowed to find its own level. With this effective devaluation, the Government's European policy was seriously embarrassed.

Opponents of Maastricht took the view that as Britain was no longer in the ERM, it could not contemplate any move to EMU and a single currency.

The devaluation and the closeness of the French result gave considerable ammunition for those in Britain who wanted to undermine the Maastricht process. The Major Government was beset by problems on several fronts, and the Tory Right and elements in the Labour Party sensed their opportunity to hold up or block the Bill altogether. They portrayed the Community as being in disarray, with a rising tide of opinion across Europe in opposition to the Treaty.

In August 1993, British ratification was completed, and in November the European Union officially came into existence. But the European issue continued to dog the Government over the following years.

Europe and the Major government 1992-1997

The Prime Minister's 'double opt-out' was initially hailed by many Conservatives as a triumph, but thereafter he had a difficult course to navigate. At the same time as he was trying to convince our partners in the European Council that he was a 'good European', he had to persuade his own right-wing that he was rolling back the influence of the Community.

After 1992, with an ever-dwindling majority, John Major was increasingly forced to adopt language and postures which seemed to be anti-European. He tried to court the known Euro-sceptics, the Euro-phobes and the jingoistic vote in the country by a series of 'tough' stances towards our European partners, particularly over revised voting arrangements in the Council of Ministers and over the choice of President for the European Commission. His remarks often sounded highly critical of the European Union, and ministers blocked measures that appeared to be integrationist in spirit. This obstructive attitude was to reach its peak during the dispute over BSE, the 'mad cow' disease which afflicted an increasing number of British cattle (see box overleaf).

By employing such tactics, John Major sacrificed some support from pro-European Conservatives (particularly the more pro-federal MEPs) who were dismayed by the policy and approach post-Maastricht. Neither did he win

The dispute over BSE

In March 1996, the British Government broke the news that there could be a link between Bovine Spongiform Encephalopathy (BSE) and a fatal human disease, Creutzfeldt-Jakob disease (CJD). The evidence it had available pointed to the danger of people contracting CJD from eating infected beef. The European Commission imposed a ban on exports of all beef and beef products throughout the world, a move which faced many British farmers with the prospect of a total collapse of their beef market. Ministers urged a lifting of the embargo in return for taking a series of measures designed to eliminate the risk of BSE in British cattle, involving the slaughter of many animals deemed to be at risk. However, many member states of the EU were less than sympathetic, fearing the spread of BSE to the continent.

British frustration at the slow progress in getting a removal of the ban led the Prime Minister to order a policy of non-cooperation in the transaction of EU business. Britain would not agree to decisions on any matters awaiting resolution in the Council, without there being a timetable for removal of embargo. The imposition of such a policy irritated EU members, even those who were more understanding about Britain's plight. They pointed out that ministers were actually holding up progress on issues such as fraud with which they were in strong sympathy. Eventually, at Florence in June 1996, the policy of non-cooperation was lifted. The ban remains, though in certain respects it has been modified.

The issue raised many questions about Britain's place in the Union. Pro-Europeans felt that if ministers had approached the Commission about the problem before they went public, it might have been 'managed' differently. They pointed out that Europe was not the problem but the solution to the problem, for the Commission was prepared to make money available for the compensation of farmers whose livelihood was at risk.

On the other hand, Euro-sceptics saw the opportunity of denouncing the Brussels machinery for its allegedly anti-British stance, and were keen to exploit anti-European feeling. In particular, the attitude of the tabloid press and many politicians over the BSE issue was rabidly jingoistic and xenophobic. Ministers sometimes and Euro-sceptics much of the time presented the argument as though hostilities had been declared, leading one prominent businessman to observe[1] that 'some among us...have failed to notice that the war with Germany has ended'.

Not surprisingly, the conflict was seen by many Europeans as just one more example of Britain being out of step with the rest of the Union. They were weary of what they saw as anti-European posturing, and longed to see a government whose ministers were willing to play a more constructive role on the continent.

The whole story illustrated how hard it was for many people in Britain to come to terms with European membership and its demands. They disliked European meddling and were convinced that the world wide ban was unnecessary, catastrophic in its impact and probably illegal. The failure of the Court of Justice to lift it served only to confirm their belief that the Court was behaving in an arbitrary and unfair manner where Britain was concerned. When it came matters involving wheeler-dealing with other states, British isolation was all too evident.

the wholehearted approval of the Thatcherite Right, many of whom were prepared to back him in any successful stand he made against the drive towards closer union. The Euro-phobes were not easily appeased, indeed they seemed to become more phobic as the Prime Minister adjusted his position. In 1995, John Redwood challenged him for the party leadership, largely on an anti-European platform, and in so doing had the backing of eight Tory MPs who had had the whip withdrawn as a result of their votes against the Government on a key European issue.

Mr Major was forced to give a high priority to questions of party unity, and like Harold Wilson in the Labour Party of the 1970s he sought to perform a balancing act. He tried to be cool and sceptical enough to win round the wavering Thatcherites, and constructive enough to keep pro-Europeans content. The attempt was not a success, and Europe proved a seriously damaging issue in the run-up to the 1997 election.

Labour in opposition and office

In the late 1980s, Labour adopted a markedly more positive tone about matters concerning Europe. This pro-European of the late 1980s stance was much influenced by Jacques Delors' advocacy of a social dimension to the activities of the European Community. Neil Kinnock and the Labour Party were attracted by what he had to say. Labour under his leadership began to work more closely with its fellow left-wing parties on the continent, some of whom were in government themselves and keen to see Britain working with them to develop the European Community.

The Smith leadership continued this new approach after the 1992 election defeat, and modernisers such as Gordon Brown and Tony Blair were always seen as sympathetic to the EC at this time. Neil Kinnock actually ended up being appointed a European Commissioner in 1994, and his wife was already proving to be an active MEP in the socialist group in the European Parliament.

The Blair era: Labour in opposition, 1994-1997

On becoming leader, Tony Blair soon made it clear that he wished Britain to play a constructive role in Europe. Back in 1975, he had voted for Britain to remain in the European Community. By inclination, this marked him out as a pro-European. However, when he entered the House of Commons in 1983, like other new Labour entrants, he absorbed the official party line espoused by Michael Foot and advocated British withdrawal from the EC - though he did enter the caveat in his personal manifesto 'unless fundamental changes are effected'. He wasn't Bennite in his opposition to the Community, but noted that it removed Britain's freedom of manoeuvre in economic policies. He didn't see Europe as a defining issue at that time, not one worth making any sort of stand about - even if he had private misgivings about his party's approach.

By the late 1980s/early 1990s, along with many other Labour members, he had come to see how useful Europe might be in reviving the fortunes of social democratic politics. He didn't need to decide in detail what he did believe about the issue, but watched with growing pleasure the turmoil it caused in Tory ranks. He was keen to see Labour a step ahead of his opponents. He was alarmed by the 'drift towards isolation in Europe', and wanted to see instead 'constructive engagement'.

Describing himself as a 'passionate European' by the time he became leader in 1994, he was alarmed by the xenophobic tone of the tabloid press. He wished to see the country 'at the centre of Europe', and wanted to see it fulfil its destiny on the continent and its 'historical role in the world'. Without being active within the Union, Britain would forfeit any chance of global influence; Europe must be 'our base'.

As Opposition leader, he sounded positive about Europe, but this did not mean that he was wildly idealistic. Indeed, he advocated reform of European institutions and of the CAP. But whilst he was intent on safeguarding national interests and ensuring that Britain got its best possible deal from the EU, he wasn't in favour of the 'impotent posturing' of the then Prime Minister.

On the **single currency**, he sounded more sympathetic than John Major. He felt that if it could be made to work, it would be a good thing, and noted its practical advantages such as greater stability, lower transaction costs and lower interest rates. His only anxiety was whether it could work in a Union in which there were serious economic discrepancies between the different regions of the Union. The approach was 'watchful EMU-readiness', not very different from the approach of pro-Europeans in the Government who wanted to 'prepare and decide'.

The Labour government 1997-?

In office, Labour made it a priority to mend fences with Europe and re-establish Britain's position on the continent. From an early stage, Tony Blair's strong Parliamentary and party position enabled him to adopt a more positive tone, and he quickly indicated that Britain would play a leading role in the Union. He signed up for the Social Chapter, was prominent in Union discussions and let it be known that Britain was likely to enter into a single currency when the convergence criteria were met - as long as the British people approved such an initiative. His intention was to use the British Presidency in the first half of 1998 to illustrate his wish for Britain to be a leading participant in any decisions concerning the evolution of the Union. His priorities in those six months were crime, jobs and the environment.

For the first time, Britain seemed to have an administration which seemed genuine in wishing to place itself 'at the heart of Europe'. It had a minister with specific responsibilities for European policy, one who could speak for Britain in intergovernmental negotiations; previously, Britain had usually been represented by a civil servant. Moreover, Robin Cook as Foreign Secretary appointed an MEP to act as his European Parliamentary Private Secretary (EPPS), and help him handle relations with the Parliament in Strasbourg.

Such concessions and the willingness to negotiate rather than confront were indicative of a genuine change in the British line. Ministers gave out positive vibrations, making it clear that they were not seeking to be obstructive. These were well-received, and there was much goodwill among European leaders to the new Government and a greater willingness to appreciate Britain's difficulties over aspects of Union policy.

The tone of the new Prime Minister's rhetoric was more pro-European than anything which had been heard by British ministers for some considerable time:

(We want) a Europe that works together as a team, in which our countries retain their distinctive identities...but work together to tackle common problems for the practical benefit of all...Our joint mission is to make Europe work for the People: a Europe that is closer to the people's priorities: peace and prosperity, progress and partnership.

The Amsterdam Summit and beyond

One of the new Prime Minister's first tasks was to attend the important Amsterdam Summit which was intended to clear up a number of outstanding issues affecting the future development of the Union. The Amsterdam Treaty was signed on June 18, 1997. Its 144 pages were ratified by the European Parliament and member countries despite alleged shortcomings.

It was widely believed that some modest progress had been made in bringing the EU closer to the people. In addition, there was:

- a positive move to tackle unemployment and boost equal opportunities
- an attempt to create greater transparency and tackle fraud
- a green light for applicant countries to press their claims for admission
- an extension to the powers of the European Parliament, its law-making role being enhanced in certain areas, as were its consultation rights on matters such as home affairs, justice and employment policy
- a slight increase in the scope for majority voting in the Council of Ministers.

Critics noted that there had been no agreement on institutional reform. If the Union was to be enlarged, the need for progress in this area was clear-cut, for without it the smooth and democratic functioning of a community of some twenty members was at risk.

The British Presidency did not achieve all that those in charge had hoped for, and in the months which followed it became apparent that there were problems ahead for ministers, not least over the thorny issue of the British rebate. However, at the Berlin European Council (May 1999) a settlement was agreed to the problems of imbalances in the net national contributions to the EU budget. As part of it, Britain was allowed to hang on to its hard-won compensation.

Tony Blair sees that agreement and the decision of the Commission to lift the ban on British beef exports to the continent, as an indication that his policy of 'constructive engagement' with our continental partners is succeeding. Using the slogan 'pro-Europe, pro-reform', he has begun to counter the 'forces of anti-Europeanism' which find expression in the speeches of some politicians and in the attitudes of many members of the public, as registered in opinion surveys. His view is that voters accept the need to be in Europe but have little enthusiasm for the project: they want the benefits of membership, but feel that it is time for the Union to get its act together and remove some of its unattractive features and unpalatable practices.

In late 1999, European policy is far less divisive within the Government and the Labour Party than it has been for a long while. At last, the question of whether Britain has a place in the Union seems to have been given a positive answer by leading figures on the Left. Some senior Conservatives are unable to agree over that basic fact, and the party today continues to agonise over the nature and extent of its European commitment. (See also p97-103).

CONCLUSION

John Major had aimed to place Britain at the heart of Europe, a challenge he took up 'with enthusiasm'. However, in the last years of Conservative Government - as in the earlier years under Margaret Thatcher - there was often a distinct coolness in the British approach. It became apparent that within the Conservative Party there was little sympathy for extending British commitments within the Union. The Prime Minister sought to limit its competence and delay making any decisions which bound Britain more closely to the other member states. Some of his supporters were even prepared to contemplate a future for Britain outside the Union.

David Butler and Martin Westlake[2] have pointed out that Euro-scepticism in Britain has a long history:

If there is a European 'problem', it is not restricted to one British political party, but more generally diffused throughout the British political and administrative establishment...In truth, virtually every post-war British Prime Minister has been in a similar position and played a similar role, from Attlee to Churchill and Eden, from Macmillan to Wilson, and from Callaghan to Major and Thatcher.

EU institutions

INTRODUCTION

There are five main institutions in the European Union and its decision-making processes. Three of these are supranational in character, and two intergovernmental.

In the second category, are the **European Council**, which provides an overall sense of direction in Union matters, and the **Council of Ministers** which adopts legislation in its final form, having taken account of Parliament's views.

In the first category, are the **European Commission** which makes legislative proposals, the **Parliament** which considers these draft proposals and where necessary amends them, and the **Court of Justice** which adjudicates in the case of disputes arising from the interpretation and application of the Treaties and of the legislation based upon them.

ASK YOURSELF

- On what grounds, if any, can the Commission be criticised?
- The European Parliament has long been portrayed as weak and ineffective. Is this still a fair assessment?
- Why do some British politicians despair of the European Court of Justice?
- Why has the European Council assumed a growing importance in recent years?
- Does real power still lay with the Council of Ministers?
- Is there a democratic deficit in the Union today? Does it matter? Can anything be done about it?

MAIN TEXT

The institutions of the European Union

i. The Council of Ministers

At the head of the European Union, making policy decisions and issuing directives like a government of the EU, is the Council of Ministers which is made up of one minister from each member country. Usually, for routine business, the minister concerned is the Foreign Minister, although when farming matters are to be discussed it is the Minister of Agriculture just as when green issues are on the agenda the Secretary of State for the Environment takes the seat. Preparations for the meetings are handled by COREPER (see p72).

Each member country in turn acts as *President of the European Union* for six months (Jan-June and July-Dec.). During those six months, all Council meetings are chaired by the relevant minister from the country holding the presidency. Austria held the Presidency in the second half of 1998, Germany and Finland in 1999, and Portugal and France assume the position in 2000.

ii. The European Council

At least once every six months there is a 'summit meeting' attended by the prime ministers of all member countries (for France the meetings are attended by the President). These are known as European Councils and they are held in the country holding the presidency at that time. They allow for discussion of broad issues, and help to move the Union forward on key issues. Agreements reached have no legislative force, but must first be turned into legislation on the basis of a proposal from the Commission in the normal way.

iii. The European Commission

The Commission is the executive of the EU, not only providing the bureaucracy like civil servants, but able to make policy decisions like government ministers. It consists of twenty Commissioners representing all 15 member countries, and an EU civil service of approximately 14,000 full-time officials who work in 26 Directorates-General each dealing with a different area of responsibility.

Each Commissioner is nominated by his or her country; e.g., Neil Kinnock is now the Vice-President, with special responsibility for internal reform and Chris Patten is the new commissioner in charge of external affairs. Once appointed, a Commissioner is expected to adopt a European attitude and not favour his or her country of origin. The Commission is appointed to serve for five years. At the head of the Commission is the *President* (formerly Jacques Delors, then Jacques Santer and now Romano Prodi), appointed by the European Council with the consent of the European Parliament. The President acts as head of government for the Union, attending European Council meetings and representing the EU at international meetings.

iv. The Court of Justice

The European Court of Justice has 15 judges and 9 Advocates-General, and is based in Luxembourg. It rules on matters of Union law as it is laid down in the various treaties setting up the component communities of the EU. It can arbitrate in disputes between member states, on those between the Commission and member states and also over-rule national law where that conflicts with Union law (see box below). It has the power to levy fines on firms found to be in breach of Union law, and on those states which fail to carry out their treaty obligations.

Types of European law

European Law deriving from the treaties is known as **Primary legislation**.

Secondary legislation includes:

Regulations (binding on all states, without the need for any national legislation)

Directives (binding as to the result to be achieved, but can be implemented as best suits member countries)

Decisions (binding on those individuals and organisations to whom they are addressed)

Recommendations and Opinions are not actually laws, and lack binding force.

There are usually in the region of 2,000-3,000 measures introduced every year, most of which are non-contentious. More than half are regulations, many more are decisions and relatively few are directives.

---

v. The European Parliament

The **European Parliament** was originally an unelected assembly. It became directly elected in 1979, with the number of MEPs from each country determined by its size. Whereas Luxembourg has six MEPs,

A powerful parliament?

Its legislative role

The legislative powers of the Parliament were initially only advisory. Under the **Consultation Procedure**, Parliament gives an opinion on Commission proposals. This still applies in areas such as the CAP, taxation and some aspects of EMU.

In the 1986 Single European Act they were extended through the **Cooperation Procedure**, which allowed the Parliament a greater say in making amendments to the Council. The Council can ultimately override the Parliament, but only on the basis of a unanimous vote.

Co-decision was introduced by the Maastricht Treaty. It gives the Parliament a right of veto over Union legislation in some key areas, and allows it as a last resort to reject proposals by an absolute majority of its members. This applies to topics such as single market measures, consumer protection, and research and development.

By the **Assent Procedure**, Parliament has to approve or reject, by simple or absolute majority, all trade, cooperation, association or membership agreements concluded between the Union and a non-member country or group of countries. If assent is withheld, the agreement cannot come into effect. As the range of agreements is very wide, this is an important addition to Parliament's powers.

Its struggle for influence

Parliament and the Commission usually have a good working relationship, but this has come under strain over some issues. MEPs have been highly critical of what they see as the failure of the Commission to tackle fraud. In a struggle over the issue in early 1999, they were on the verge of sacking the twenty Commissioners because of their dissatisfaction with the action being taken by Jacques Santer. Although numerous cases of fraud and mismanagement had been uncovered and some officials dismissed or downgraded, no action was taken against two Commissioners who were in the firing line because of their alleged abuse of their position. If Parliament voted to censure individual Commissioners, Santer let it be known that his entire team would resign, a move which could paralyse much of the work of the whole Commission. Faced with the choice of either voting to remove the twenty or climbing down, Parliament - having shown its teeth - backed off. Its power of dismissal is a blunt one, an all-or-nothing solution, and because of this it is unlikely to be much employed.

Germany now has 99. The full Parliament meets in Strasbourg one week in every month, with debates, question time and reports from Commissioners, but much of the important work is done in one of the 20 all-party standing committees which are based in Brussels and take up two weeks in every month. The main powers of the European Parliament (EP) are:

- To vote on the acceptance of new member states
- To reject or amend Council decisions affecting the Single Market
- To reject or amend the EU budget
- To dismiss the entire Commission, on a two-thirds majority
- To accept or reject a new President of the Commission.

MEPs work within European party groups of which the two largest are the **Party of European Socialists (PES)** on the Left (this includes the British Labour Party), and the **European People's Party (EPP)** on the Centre-Right (this is largely made up of Christian Democrats but the Conservative Party is allied to the EPP).

Elections to the European Parliament

The Treaty of Rome (Article 138) laid down that there should be proposals for 'election by direct universal suffrage, in accordance with a uniform procedure in all member states'. As yet, no such uniform system has been adopted, and until the advent of the Blair Government Britain clung to its First Past the Post (FPTP) method. The other countries have always used some variety of proportional representation.

The method of election within the EU is under review to see if the requirement of the Rome Treaty can be fulfilled. Parliament voted in favour of a new, common system back in 1991. It was agreed that it would work on producing a scheme, with the emphasis on producing the principles rather than the details of any new arrangement. The Council will have to reach unanimous agreement before any scheme is accepted, and at Maastricht provision was made for the Parliament to approve, on a majority-basis, any system which it adopts before it can be introduced. In March 1993, the European Parliament again voted for a uniform system, but there was no agreement at Council level.

The British voting system, 1979-1994

The case for a change of system in Britain was a strong one. The 87 constituencies in the United Kingdom were inevitably very large, with typical electorates of 700,000. The size factor made the outcome even more distorted than in the case in elections to the House of Commons. The outcome of the elections in 1994 well illustrated the anomalies that could occur under FPTP:

Labour had won 74% of the seats on the basis of only 44% of the vote, thereby providing it with the largest single delegation of any national party in the European Parliament. For small parties, inevitably FPTP was bad news. Although the Lib Dems gained representation for the first time, they were very unfairly treated on a proportional basis. Five years earlier, the British Greens had won 14.9% of the vote but lacked any voice in Strasbourg.

1994 results

	% Votes	Seats won
Conservatives	27	18
Labour	44	62
Lib Dems	16	2
Greens	3	0
Plaid Cymru	1	0
SNP	3	2

Such anomalies were thought by many commentators to be the more unacceptable because the European Parliament was supposed to be a deliberative forum in which differing shades of opinion were reflected. It may be the case that FPTP for Westminster is preferable, in that it usually produces a government with a working majority. No government has to be formed out of the assembly in Strasbourg, and so arguments about PR leading to coalitions were irrelevant. Similarly, the objection that multi-member constituencies would lessen the contact between an MP and his constituents had less force in these elections, for the 87 areas were already so large that any such personal connection was out of the question; such was the remoteness that few British people knew the name of their Euro-MP at present.

It was also argued that an electoral system which catered for all shades of opinion might produce a higher turnout. In other countries, turnout was invariably better than in Britain, the only exceptions being the Netherlands and Portugal in 1994.

A new system

With such considerations in mind and in fulfilment of a pre-election agreement with the Liberal Democrats, Labour made it a priority to legislate for a new electoral system in time for the 1999 elections. It committed itself to the principle of proportionality, and the Home Secretary introduced a bill to provide for its chosen form of proportional representation, based on a regional list. Jack Straw stressed the need to get women and ethnic minority candidates standing in the elections. He pointed out that prior to that election there were 'no women north of the Humber and in areas with quite a high ethnic minority concentration there are no ethnic minority candidates'.

The European Parliamentary Elections Act, 1999, provided for a list system based on larger multi-member regions for England, Scotland and Wales. Northern Ireland was exempted from the change. The then Northern Ireland Secretary, Mo Mowlam, had argued to keep the existing system with which the peoples of the province had become familiar; this was already a proportional system, the single transferable vote.

Under the new arrangements, political party lists would appear on the ballot paper together with the names of the parties' candidates. Ministers opted for the 'closed list' variety of PR, and any independent candidate was to appear under his/her own name. Voters were asked to be asked to mark one cross, either for a party list or an independent candidate. Once the votes were counted, seats would be allocated according to the proportion of the vote obtained for each party. The successful candidates would be those at the top of the list, equal to the number of seats the party won.

This exercise would be conducted in each of the constituencies. There was to be one for each of Scotland and Wales (with eight and five members respectively), whereas England would have nine regions using the same boundaries currently employed by the Government Offices for the regions, the exception being the unification of Merseyside and North West into a single area.

Criticism centred on the fact that the new system would end the right of the voters to choose an individual party candidate, although at present they have no choice to express a preference for, say, a New Labour or Old Labour candidate. An open list would have enabled them to rearrange the order of a party's list of candidates, according to their choice. Under the Government's arrangements, parties rather than voters have the greater say over which individual politicians actually end up in Strasbourg. They are in a better position to exercise more control over candidates when it comes to ranking them on the pre-selected lists.

Straw defended the Closed List system, claiming that:

i. it was a 'simple, straightforward system which takes individual candidates and allows the public to vote for particular parties. It still asks the electorate to put a single cross on the ballot paper'.

ii. it was the system used in most other large states in the EU, including France, Germany and Spain. Therefore, if adopted in Britain, it would be the system used to elect no less than 70% of the members of the Parliament.

iii. it was the best way of promoting gender equality, e.g., by alternating men and women on a list.

It was certainly an additional attraction for Tony Blair that there was a chance to reform and modernise the list of MEPs. The Prime Minister owed his party's representatives in Strasbourg no favours at all, for they had used their privileged position to embarrass the leadership. He was of the opinion that they were massively out of touch with prevailing thinking in the New Labour era.

The new closed list system: a summary

- European Parliament constituencies previously electing one member replaced by large multi-member ones (e.g., Scotland now one giant constituency instead of eight).

- Electors vote not for an individual candidate but for a party list of candidates.

- Seats in the new multi-member constituencies divided between parties according to the proportion of the vote each has gained in the constituency.

- Seats allocated to individuals according to their placing on the party list.

Turnout in 1999

Hopes of a higher turnout did not materialise. Across the Union, there was a decline in popular participation, but in Britain the lack of interest was startling. Only 23.6% of the electorate voted.

There are several possible explanations for this low figure. Labour spokespersons saw it as a reflection of broad satisfaction with the Government; as voters were contented, they felt no need to turn out. Some party activists were less complacent and noted the disillusion of Labour's core voters over the handling of social issues. Conservatives, not surprisingly, suggested that the low-key Labour campaign and the lack of leadership from the Prime Minister were to blame. They recognised that their own supporters had been less reluctant to go to the polls. Of course, Conservatives may have felt they had something to vote against, for the party campaigned strongly against British membership of the Euro - on which Labour ministers had little to say.

Whatever view is correct, there is the stark fact that many British people feel uninterested in and disengaged from the whole European project. They generally see a reason for being in the Union, but care little about it or for the policies it advances.

The result in 1999

Across Europe there was a swing to the Right, a trend apparent in the British result. **Labour** was destined to lose seats on a substantial scale because of the choice of electoral system. In the event it would have done even worse under FPTP. It received a trouncing as Labour voters stayed away in droves. The turnout was markedly worse in traditional Labour areas (18%) than in Middle England (23%) or the Tory heartlands (28%), suggesting that for some reason Labour voters did not feel stirred to vote.

The **Conservatives** did well, far better than they might have anticipated. They improved dramatically on their performance in the 1994 Euro elections, the 1997 general election and the 1999 council/devolved elections.

The **Liberal Democrats** won 10 seats, giving them worthwhile representation in Strasbourg. But the increase was achieved on a popular vote of only 12.5%. Their vote was squeezed by the impressive outcome for the smaller parties. They lost votes to the United Kingdom Independence Party in the South West, to the Greens in London and the South East and to the Conservatives in Scotland. 'Others' clearly did well, for 35.5% of the votes in England, Scotland and Wales went to parties ranging from those mentioned to the much less successful British National Party and Pro-European Conservatives.

In spite of the use of the list method, the two main parties still received a bonus from the electoral system. The Conservative and Labour parties both received a higher number of seats than their vote entitled them to on a strictly arithmetical basis, though the Conservative victory would have been substantially larger if FPTP had been employed. The Liberal Democrats on this occasion only marginally suffered from the electoral system. By contrast, the Greens and the UKIP between them won 13% of the popular vote but half that proportion of seats.

Critics of proportional representation are keen to cite the low turnout as evidence that voters did not understand or favour the new proportional system. It is certainly true that there was little enthusiasm for this particular variety of PR, and it may well be that some alternative method will be employed in 2004.

The actual result
England, Scotland and Wales

	% Votes	No. of Seats Won	% Seats
Conservatives	35.3	36	42.9
Labour	27.7	29	34.5
Liberal Democrats	12.5	10	11.9

NB In addition, three seats were won by UKIP, and 2 each by the Green, Plaid Cymru and the SNP

A costly parliament?

The European Parliament has its critics who often dismiss it as not only an irrelevance, but an expensive one at that. Every work spoken and every document produced has to be translated into several languages, and such costs account for almost 40% of its budget.

Though full sittings are held in Strasbourg, most committees meet in Brussels, and the Secretariat is based in Luxembourg. This is costly, as well as being inconvenient for Euro-MPs. Some 12% of expenditure is caused by this division of location. (Each month, the Parliament has to transport a mass of paperwork for the 500 mile round trip between Strasbourg and Luxembourg.)

Salaries and expenses use up much of the rest of the money. The salaries of MEPs vary between member-state. They are fixed at the level of those of their national counterparts, so that French and German ones are much

The salaries and perquisites of MEPs

At the Cardiff Summit in mid-1998, Tony Blair launched a scathing attack on the 'gravy train' which enabled some assiduous or inventive MEPs to make well over £100,000 a year on top of their salaries. He flayed the lavish benefits to which they were entitled, claiming that they undermined the credibility of all elected members.

MEPs are paid at the same rate as members in their national parliaments, which means some receive up to five times as much as colleagues sitting next to them. At the time, the Italians got the most - the equivalent of £80,000 a year - whilst the Greeks fared particularly badly, struggling along on about £15,000.

Partly to compensate for the discrepancies, expenses are lavish. There is a daily attendance allowance of £157 for signing-on; until recently, MEPs could sign the register and then leave immediately. Other benefits include:
- funding for research and secretarial assistance (£6,400)
- a communications allowance, relating to the purchase and operation of office equipment
- an allowance for travel around the world to investigate relevant problems (£2,100)

Best of all for MEPs, there are allowances for travel from constituency home to meetings in Brussels, and the monthly sessions in Strasbourg. It is this element of the expenses which enables members to so generously supplement their incomes. Some senior British MEPs estimate that they can make up to £800 a month tax-free on such journeys, but other members claim vastly more inflated amounts. They are able to claim the full cost of fares without providing any proof that they have actually paid the full rate, and can cross the road from their apartments in Brussels to attend meetings and then insist that they have driven from their constituencies in a far-flung part of the continent.

The ruses are well-known in Europe, and are supported by many MEPs who see them as a means of offsetting the disparities in their salaries. They also help to compensate members for arduous and complicated journeys associated with their work.

The Prime Minister urged the need for an open, fair and transparent means of remuneration. But when MEPs had a chance shortly afterwards to vote to limit their claims to the real cost of their journeys, they voted by 244-214 in favour of retaining the present system.

NB All figures quoted relate to those prevailing in early 1999.

better paid than British or Irish representatives. Allowances are generous for secretarial costs, research and travel, and stories of large sums being paid have fed the imagination of some critics who condemn the European 'gravy train' (see box above). The perks of being an MEP are good, the lifestyle is very comfortable, though for these rewards members have to be prepared to undertake a great deal of travelling.

With an annual budget of over £500m and a staff of nearly 3,500 officials, the Parliament is expensive to run, but not unreasonably so. Compared to other assemblies on the international scene, the cost does not seem excessive. The American House of Representatives is of similar size, meets in one location and employs only one language - yet it spends twice as much. (It does, of course, also exercise much greater power.)

Other institutions

These include:

- the **Council of Permanent Representatives of Member States (COREPER)**, which prepares work for the Council and carries out other task assigned to it. The national ambassadors who belong to COREPER are accorded the power to speak and act on behalf of their member countries on many matters of secondary significance
- the **Court of Auditors** whose task it is to audit all revenue and expenditure of the Union, and assist Parliament and the Council in checking the implementation of the annual budget
- the **Economic and Social committee (ESC)** has an advisory role, in that it gives opinions to the Council of Ministers on any proposal. Its membership reflects the various interests (e.g., unions and employers) who make up the economic and social life of the Union
- the **Committee of the Regions** made up of people representing each area of their country, to voice regional concerns. It must be consulted by the Council on matters affecting regional policy
- an **Ombudsman** to look into instances of maladministration by any EU institution.

Britain and European institutions: a summary of membership
Britain has the following representation:

1/15	in the European Council
1/15	in the Council of Ministers
1/15	on the Court of Justice
1/15	in COREPER
1/15	on the Court of Auditors
2/20	on the Commission
87/626	in the European Parliament
24/222	on the Economic and Social Committee
24/222	on the Committee of the Regions

The lack of democracy in the European Union?

When Monnet and his co-founders launched the ECSC and then formulated the Rome Treaty, they were not primarily concerned with the issue of democratic legitimacy. Yet he always envisaged[1] a move towards democratisation, and described his task as '...to ensure that in their limited field the new institutions were thoroughly democratic...the Assembly should be elected by universal suffrage within a federal system...In this way, the pragmatic method we had adopted would also lead to a federation validated by the people's vote'.

Yet Monnet and others of the period had a tendency towards elitism within their approach, and tended to assume that for the while they knew best what was needed to bring about peace and prosperity in Europe. As Holland remarks[2]: 'Europe was being constructed by a cohesive and remarkably small elite; while public support was welcomed, it was never a prerequisite for Monnet's Europe'. Democracy was slow to materialise, and until 1979 those who sat in the Strasbourg assembly were selected from the membership of their national legislatures.

The democratic deficit today

There is still no very credible system of democratic control within the Union. There is no effective accountability of the Council or Commission to either national parliaments or to the European one. This is why critics (and also often supporters) of the EU speak of its glaring 'democratic deficit'.

Sir Leon Brittan, the former senior British Commissioner, identified[3] three factors in the 'widespread sense of unease':
- The feeling that Brussels was interfering where it should not do so
- The lack of knowledge of what was going on in the key decision-making bodies
- The belief that Brussels lacked sufficient democratic legitimacy.

To correct these perceived failings, he recognised the need for the vigorous pursuit of initiatives in three areas, subsidiarity (devolution of decision-making to the most appropriate tier of government), transparency (more open and accessible decision-making) and democracy (correction of the democratic deficit).

Correcting the democratic deficit

By the democratic deficit, we mean the lack of democracy and accountability in the decision-making processes of the European Union. Philip Norton has defined[4] it as 'the limited input into the law-making processes of the European Union by directly elected representatives of the people'. He sees three solutions to the problem, namely:

i. Strengthening the powers of the European Parliament
ii. Creating a new EU institution comprising elected representatives from national parliaments
iii. Strengthening the role of national parliaments, in the law-making process.

Control via the European Parliament

The past weakness and present limitations of the European Parliament have already been described (see p64). But it is already more than an advisory body and its powers could be increased further, as the majority of MEPs wish to see happen. Any such extension of its current role is, however, highly contentious.

As yet, in Norton's phrase, the Parliament is 'still only on the edge of constituting a legislature'. Moreover, its legitimacy, enhanced in 1979 by direct elections, still suffers because of the modest turnout on each of the occasions when the European public has been invited to exercise its judgement. In Britain, far more people vote in national elections than in European ones. Observers sometimes disagree on whether it is better to enhance the powers and status of the Strasbourg Parliament in the expectation that this will stimulate interest, or whether to await evidence of popular enthusiasm before granting any increase in powers.

It is ironic that some of those in Britain who lament the 'democratic deficit' are those who are most reluctant to make the European Parliament a more effective watchdog. The Major Government was strongly opposed to any extension of the powers of the European Parliament, and saw a need for control to remain firmly in Westminster hands.

Control via a new European parliamentary institution

This approach was urged by Leon Brittan, who felt that '...if voters felt their local MPs were lending a hand to the process of Euro-legislation, it would greatly strengthen the EU's democracy and enhance its credibility'. One way of achieving this goal would be the creation of an upper house or senate, made up of people from either chamber in their national state. One of the problems is that this would create a rival body to the existing European Parliament which is still seeking to establish a greater role for itself. Any such creation might be seen to represent a dilution of the position and importance of the existing body. The outcome may be two relatively weak bodies, instead of one which is becoming more effective.

Control via national parliaments

From the 1980s onwards, most legislatures have made greater provision for dealing with European legislation and given their MPs or deputies more opportunities to acquire specialised information. In Britain, apart from the committees which have been established (see p86-87), there are rare occasions when MEPs are invited to meet with their national colleagues in party committee meetings and informally. Yet keeping up with the burden of work coming from Brussels is a difficult task for the British Parliament, and one which has grown with the preparation for and implementation of the single market. If eventually much foreign and security policy, as well as immigration and policing, are handled in Brussels the task will be even more daunting.

Other possible moves to greater democracy

To tackle the democratic deficit, the institutions of the Union must be placed under proper democratic control. Almost certainly this does mean a much greater role for the **European Parliament**, with more decisions being made subject to its approval. In other words, there is likely to be an extension of the machinery of co-decision. Some would argue that another way of making Parliament strong is to make it more representative by the adoption of a uniform voting procedure. This would make it more accurately reflect popular opinion.

Another approach is to seek to democratise the **Commission**, by making it more responsible to the Parliament, as is the case in other democratic systems. A start was made at Maastricht, in the provision that the Commission's appointment should be subject to Parliamentary approval. This idea could be taken further. Parliament could be made responsible for the initial choice of the Commission, so that it would no longer comprise nominees of individual states. Instead, it would be an executive chosen to reflect the particular balance of the assembly. In this way, elections to the Parliament would also, in effect, become elections to choose the body which initiates legislation.

A different route to the one just outlined would be to allow the public to vote for the Union's Commissioners rather than allowing them to be appointed by the national governments subject to the Parliament's approval. This could be done by the public being invited to elect one or two Commissioners in each country, on the day of the EP elections. Such direct election would provide the Commission with a powerful popular base, and enable it to share power with the Council.

Openness and transparency are similarly important, as an annex to the Maastricht Treaty clearly established;
The Conference considers that transparency of the decision-making process strengthens the democratic nature of the institutions and the public's confidence in the administration.

The Council has changed its rules of procedure. Although debates are still held in secret, there is now more information available about the way in which states voted, with some explanation as to the events which led up to the final outcome. However, access to documents is still limited. More could also be done to ensure that legislation is intelligible and clearly drafted, and to consolidate laws on various areas of policy.

A former French President, Giscard d'Estaing, has urged the need for concerted action to rectify the 'democratic deficit':
The Community cannot continue to be governed according to procedures which are contrary to the imperative requirements it formulates itself in relation to countries which are candidates for membership.

His remarks are echoed by many politicians and commentators. Certainly, EU support for new democratic states in Central and Eastern Europe lies uneasily with its own barely democratic system of control of Union decision-making institutions. Democratisation of a Union in the process of becoming a more federal state and lying at the heart of a wider European unity seems to be an idea whose time has come.

CONCLUSION

Decision-making in the EU can be carried out by several different processes. They are little known other than to those whose work is associated with the Union, and the institutions involved seem remote to many citizens. This sense of remoteness and lack of understanding lead many observers, especially in Britain, to conclude that too much power is centralised in Brussels and that the European Commission in particular poses a serious threat to the authority of the national government at Westminster.

The problem is recognised by some people who work within the Union. In the evidence it presented to the Reflections Group in 1995, the Commission itself observed that:
a union that is closer to the people has to be a Union where decisions are easier to comprehend, whose actions are better justified, whose responsibilities are clearer and whose legislation is more accessible.

Subsidiarity and greater openness are two solutions often put forward, but as yet the latter in particular has made little substantial impact on the workings of the Union. It is anxiety about the way the institutions function which inspires even some politicians sympathetic to the EU to call for change (see box opposite). Institutional reform in any case is going to be

Two views of EU institutional reform

In mid-1998, Paddy Ashdown, leader of the Liberal Democrats, and Robin Cook, Foreign Secretary, put forward their views on the way forwards for the Union.

Paddy Ashdown

argued[5] that people across Europe are in the dark about an organisation increasingly responsible for key decisions affecting their lives. The European Union speaks a language few can understand, 'that inscrutable, acronym-laden bureaucratic-speak which dominates so much communication in the EU'. He also excoriated the EU for its invisibility, citing the Council of Ministers' habit of meeting in secret behind closed doors.

Among his solutions are:
- an assault on 'the culture of secrecy' with a demand for a Freedom of Information Charter for all EU bodies
- additional teeth for the Parliament, enabling it to hold the 'over-mighty Commission and Council to account'
- a written constitution for the EU, formulated from the bottom up, a radical departure for a body which has long been run from the top down, as the exclusive preserve of the great European elites.

The advantages of a written, accessible constitution, contained in a single document - clear enough to be understood by everybody and short enough to be easily carried around - are that it *would strip away the mystique of the EU. Most people cannot comb through the sub-clauses of the Treaty of Rome; they deserve to have the rules of this new, seem-government spelled out, in black and white. In an instant, the EU would seem less faceless and out of reach, and more like a human-made creation that can be moulded and changed...A written constitution would help break down the sense of alienation.*

Robin Cook is also concerned about the democratic deficit that separates European institutions from the people they are meant to represent. He says[6] they seem remote, and beyond the reach of citizens in member states. His solution is to involve those bodies which do have a hold on voters' allegiances, chiefly national parliaments, in the democratic work of Europe, a radical departure in Union policy. He proposes the creation of a second chamber in Europe, made up of MPs from national parliaments, to curb the power of Brussels. The chamber would sift through decisions made in Brussels and block any that meddle in the minutiae of British life.

The idea is aimed at involving MPs directly in the running of the Union: 'Our Parliament needs to be part of the project rather than outside of it...The European Parliament does a very useful job, but the missing link is tying the national parliaments with the work of Europe'. Others take a different view, and feel that the body which should hold this European executive to account is the European Parliament. If directly-elected MEPs had genuine powers of scrutiny, this would erase the democratic deficit in an instant.

Robin Cook would probably argue that the problem is that the

European Parliament lacks public esteem, that it is national parliaments which are respected. This may be true, but if MEPs were given political muscle voters might then learn to take them more seriously.

Robin Cook also argues for a new code on subsidiarity within the EU to clarify those subjects which are best dealt with at European level, leaving the rest to national, regional or local government. A recent think-tank report[7] has given some backing to this idea, noting that most European citizens want to see the development of clear capabilities to deal with those areas - including crime, environmental protection, unemployment and peace-keeping - which they see as clearly requiring an international approach. They do not want a burgeoning of some kind of super-state institutions, and a fresh look at subsidiarity could be useful in setting out what tasks other than these are better done in each country at the appropriate tier.

essential if enlargement occurs over the coming years, for decision-making in a community of more than twenty states is unlikely to operate smoothly under the present arrangements. Although little progress was made in Amsterdam to address the issues seriously, the topic will return to the agenda in the not-too-distant future. As always, one of the major barriers to effective reform will be the sturdy (some would say stubborn) defence of national interests exhibited by representatives of some countries who are reluctant or unwilling to compromise.

The impact of the EU on government and politics

INTRODUCTION

Membership of the European Union has had an important impact on the British Constitution, and on the political life of the last twenty five years. With the passing of the Single European Act and the signing of the Maastricht Treaty, the trend towards more decision-making in Brussels has accelerated. In the process, many aspects of our political and constitutional arrangements have been modified, and some of the most important effects have been those concerning the Constitution and Parliament.

ASK YOURSELF

- How does membership of the European Union affect the doctrine of Parliamentary Sovereignty?
- Which treaties or laws associated with the European Union have done most to undermine that sovereignty?
- To what extent has power been taken away from British politicians?
- How has Parliament sought to adjust to the demands of EU membership?
- Is Europe re-writing the British Constitution?

MAIN TEXT

The impact on the constitution

For many years, the British Constitution provoked little academic analysis. Textbook writers showed how the Constitution had gradually evolved and adapted over a long era, and debate concentrated on the extent to which it was written or unwritten.

Since the 1970s, there has been much discussion of the need for constitutional renewal, with the growth of groups such as Charter 88 calling for a written constitution and other fundamental changes. Since coming to office, Labour has devolved power, embraced proportional representation for European elections and incorporated the European Convention on Human Rights, among other things. Constitutional change is in the air, and any changes now introduced are initiated against the background of British membership of the European Union. This has had a profound impact already on the workings of the British Constitution, and any re-casting of relations with the EU could have further effects.

On entering the Community, for the first time an external body could override Parliament, and anti-Europeans have often deployed the sovereignty argument in support of the case. Enoch Powell, a trenchant Tory critic of British membership, emphasised that sovereignty cannot be pooled, for it means 'final and absolute authority within the political community'. Either you have it or you do not. Therefore, sovereignty was incompatible with membership, as for the first time Community law would take precedence over any Parliamentary statute.

Ministers denied this at the time of Accession and in the 1975 Referendum. They detected no erosion of sovereignty, and the 1975 referendum 'Yes' pamphlet claimed that 'no important new policy can be decided in Brussels or anywhere else without the consent of a British minister answerable to a British government and parliament'.

Nonetheless, the White Paper issued at the time of the 1975 Referendum explained other implications of membership. On joining, Britain agreed to 43 volumes of existing legislation, including 2,900 regulations and 410 directives already passed by the Community. These became part of British law. The then Prime Minister, Harold Wilson, stressed that accession and continued membership involved:

The acceptance in advance as part of the law of the United Kingdom, of provisions to be made in the future by instruments issued by the Community institutions - a situation for which there is no precedent in this country. It would also involve that in the fields occupied by the Community law, Parliament would have to refrain from passing fresh legislation inconsistent with that law...

This was a substantial modification to the Sovereignty of Parliament, the doctrine which has often been seen as the linch-pin of the Constitution for nearly three hundred years. A sovereign Parliament acknowledges no restraint on its powers, and can pass legislation without fear of being over-ridden. There are theoretically no legal limits to the power of Parliament, which can make or unmake any law, and no Parliament can bind another.

The debate about loss of Parliamentary Sovereignty is a contentious one. Much of Parliament's power had been ceded to the Executive well before Britain joined the EEC, in part a reflection of the general decline of legislatures and the increasing power of governments in many democratic countries. In other words, in practice political sovereignty already rested firmly in the Executive branch.

Lord Hailsham noted this trend back in 1976, when he used the phrase the 'elective dictatorship' to describe the operation of British government. He pointed out that the sovereignty of Parliament was in reality the sovereignty of a government elected by a minority of the voters. Armed with a Parliamentary majority which enabled them to push legislation through the House of Commons, ministers could use the whips as necessary to insist on loyalty in the voting lobbies.

The supremacy of European Law: Factortame and beyond

It was Lord Denning, a distinguished British judge, who remarked that Community legislation would be like an incoming tide which would wash away the traditional common law of Britain. What had always been known as the theoretical situation was amply demonstrated in the Factortame Case, described overleaf. As *The Economist* said at the time: 'The Europeans are re-writing our Constitution'.

What had been a potential possibility was now seen as a fait accompli. However, Philip Norton has pointed out[1] that really the significant date was before that judgement. It was the passage of the SEA, for when Britain accept Qualified Majority Voting (QMV) it meant that British law could be changed by Brussels directives, even though the British might oppose them. What had been a national veto over proposals was removed in certain areas of policy at a stroke.

Factortame

The supremacy of European over national law has been made clear on a number of subsequent occasions such as that involving the dispute with the Spanish fishermen. They were evading an agreement on fishing quotas by using British-registered vessels to fish in UK waters. The British Government responded by passing the Merchant Shipping Act of 1988 which laid down a strict definition of what made a vessel qualify as British. After a series of challenges in the European Court, it was decided that the Act contradicted EC law because it was discriminatory in a Community which was committed to freedom of movement. The effect was to establish that British courts can suspend British legislation if they believe that Community law is being infringed.

The Sovereignty of Parliament was undermined in a different way by the staging of the 1975 Referendum, the first national one ever held in Britain. The issue of whether to accept the renegotiated terms and stay in the Community or reject them and pull out, was put to the people for their verdict. The same Prime Minister referred to above explained that Parliament would accept the verdict of the people as binding. In other words, Parliament was not in reality making the decision, even if it would have to pass any necessary legislation to leave the EC. (The referendum also provoked another breach with traditional constitutional practice. Collective Responsibility was waived, in recognition of the divisions within the Government over Britain's future in Europe. Ministers did not have to agree 'to tell the same story' to the public).

The impact on the Courts

British judges have acquired a wider role, for they can now interpret Union law as well as enforce national legislation. As Lord Scarman put it back in 1974:

We are this moment part of a legal system which not only confers a right but imposes a duty on the Court in certain circumstances to invalidate legislation.

Indeed, within the British Constitution, Norton has detected[2] a shift in power among the institutions. British judges now seem less reluctant to challenge governments than in the past, and in the 1980s and 1990s did so freely. This reflects the trend on the continent where judges are more politically engaged. Several of our judges seem to have become more European-minded in their approach, and in particular more 'rights-conscious'.

Membership has had an effect on the rights of individuals. It has played a role in seeking to achieve equal treatment for men and women, and in some cases the British Government has had to back down and allow British workers rights which are supported by the Union, in areas such as social security and equal opportunities. Enforcement of rights can be a slow business, but citizens have gained another avenue through which they can be protected.

Impact on the Executive

At the highest level, the Prime Minister and Cabinet have regular dealings with the European Union. Some government departments are particularly involved in EU policy, and the relevant Secretaries of State will from time to time attend or even chair meetings of the Council of Ministers. The Prime Minister has a key role in the European Council. In Cabinet and Cabinet Committee discussions, European issues often require discussion, and ministers much involved in the situation sit on a special committee chaired by the Foreign Secretary.

Officials in Whitehall are also much involved in European work. At the top of the hierarchy, the Cabinet Office is especially relevant, its senior figures attending all inter-departmental meetings on European matters. Within government departments - ranging from the Treasury to Trade, from agriculture to employment - there are special European sections, and the inter-departmental committee structure of permanent and ad hoc gatherings co-ordinates the handling of policy matters.

After years in which its status was in decline, the Foreign Office has become more powerful in recent years. In many of the leading ministerial disputes of the Thatcher period, the Prime Minister was frustrated by the pro-European stance adopted by Foreign Secretaries such as Sir Geoffrey Howe and Douglas Hurd, and the advisers who influenced their thinking.

The impact on the Legislature

We have seen that the Sovereignty of Parliament has been affected by membership. So has its workload, for by the early 1990s some 800 proposals were being initiated by the European Commission. Many of these are relatively unimportant, but the time available in both Houses of Parliament to sift and scrutinise them is inevitably limited. When Commission proposals are sent to the Council of Ministers, the relevant British government department prepares a summary and sends this to the two Houses.

In the House of Lords there is a Select Committee on the European Communities whose 24 members consider all Union proposals, and report to the House on those which raise important questions of principle or policy. There are six permanent sub-committees, which deal with matters such as Agriculture and Food, and the Environment. They co-opt other Peers to help them on specialised matters from time to time, and altogether about 80 members are involved in this work.

Of the 800 or so proposals, about half are sent to the sub-committees for further investigation. Many are merely noted, but about one in ten are more thoroughly examined; about twenty reports are issued each year. The reports of the Select Committee are highly regarded and are made available to the European Parliament where they are usually seen as thorough and illuminating. In addition to the Committee's proceedings, the Lords hold debates on European matters and some Peers have a further involvement by doubling as MEPs. Like the reports, other proceedings in the House tend to be ignored by the popular media.

In the House of Commons, the Select Committee on European Legislation acts as a filter for the Commission's proposals, and it draws the attention of the House to those which require further debate. There is a Resolution of the House (passed in 1990) which asserts that when a proposal goes from the Commission to the Council the relevant British minister will not approve the measure until it has been considered by the appropriate parliamentary committee:

In the opinion of this House, no minister of the Crown should give agreement in the Council of Ministers to any proposal for European Community legislation which is still subject to scrutiny (that is, on which the Select

Committee on European Legislation has not completed its scrutiny); or which is awaiting consideration by the House.

The Government makes time available to consider reports of the Select Committee, though there have been criticisms that debates often get a low priority in the timetable and are relegated to late evening when the House may be poorly attended. Such complaints about the inadequate opportunities to examine European legislation are commonly heard in other EU countries; all of them have difficulty in coping with the immense volume of Union work. In Britain, the task is more difficult because Parliamentary sessions do not coincide with the European working year, and this means that issues which surface in the recess can escape scrutiny.

The House of Commons tackled this dissatisfaction in 1991 by agreeing to establish two permanent Standing Committees. These examine any documentation from the EU which has been recommended for further consideration by the House. However, for all of the complaints from backbenchers about inadequate scrutiny of Brussels initiatives, most of them are unenthusiastic about personally becoming involved in closer examination. It was not easy to find twenty six MPs willing to serve on the two new bodies.

In the end, the scrutiny process does nothing to prevent the implementation of Union legislation, the committees being concerned to deal with prospective legislation only. Parliament cannot amend or revise legislation that has already passed through the European legislative process.

The House also tackles European issues in debates and at Question Time, and a Bill such as that ratifying Maastricht is necessarily a time-consuming one. Because control over European policy is inevitably limited, some commentators argue that the Strasbourg Parliament needs to be strengthened to ensure that there is real accountability within the Union (seep74-75).

The impact on devolved and local government

As a highly centralised unitary state, Britain has been reluctant in recent years to devolve power to the regions of Britain. At the local level, institutions were weakened in the Conservative era after 1979, and a proliferation of non-elected, centrally-appointed agencies assumed many powers previously exercised by councils.

Yet the Maastricht Treaty placed much emphasis on the idea of subsidiarity which says that government should be conducted at the lowest level appropriate for the performance of particular tasks. Indeed, John Major made a virtue of his resistance to the centralising powers of Brussels, and portrayed his advocacy of subsidiarity as a triumph for British democracy, marking the time when Britain began to roll back the tide.

The logic of subsidiarity appears to have important implications for regional and local government, but during the Tory years there was no concession to the demands for greater autonomy made in Scotland and Wales. Until the Maastricht Treaty, both countries were forced to present their case in Europe via the overall UK machinery. The creation of an advisory Committee of the Regions provided a new outlet for their representatives, and offices were established in Brussels in order to provide better opportunities for lobbying EU institutions. Advice was taken from representatives of the powerful German Lander governments which had long had regional ambassadors there.

Without any established machinery of regional government, other areas of UK were potentially at some disadvantage. But larger local authorities in England showed interest in defending their interests via Europe, and a number of them established special departments dealing with European affairs; some even set up an office in Brussels. Councils such as Birmingham and Huddersfield have seized the opportunity to press their claims for EU funding for major civic projects.

In one other respect, local authorities have been affected by the EU machinery. Much Union legislation introduces regulations requiring a monitoring of standards in areas such as consumer protection and the environment, and some authorities have been very effective in rising to the challenge presented to them in implementing this kind of proposal.

The election of a Labour government has created a climate in which subsidiarity could acquire a new meaning. The recently-established parliaments in Scotland and Wales and the creation of regional machinery have opened up new possibilities and may help to give the areas of Britain a larger role in the developing Europe of the Regions. Those elected can be expected to make common cause with their counterparts from the Lander and the Spanish autonomous regions.

CONCLUSION

The European dimension to British politics is now well-established and it has affected almost every aspect of the political landscape. Institutions as well as policies have been adjusted to meet the demands of entry and of the subsequent agreements made with other EU countries. Membership of the European Union now constitutes one of the leading features of the Constitution. Two changes - the Single European Act and the Maastricht Treaty - have not only altered the balance of power within the Union; they have also effected a change in the relationship between national states such as Britain and the institutions of the EU, especially via the extension of majority voting.

....

Among the most interesting political effects of membership of the EU on Britain have been those concerning the four 'P's, parties, politicians, pressure groups and the public, all of which are considered in the following four chapters.

Political parties and Europe

INTRODUCTION

The issue of Britain's relationship with Europe, and particularly with the European Union, has been a difficult one for the two main parties. In the last decade or so, the Conservatives have found the issue to be seriously divisive, whilst previously it was the Labour Party which suffered serious internal ructions because of it.

Initially, the dispute over Europe was over the issue of membership of the European Community. For a long while this has not been the case, although some politicians and observers do make occasional calls for withdrawal. In recent years, the questions for the parties have concerned the form the Union should take, and how to react to the initiatives and policies espoused by leading figures in other EU countries. Today, New Labour ministers are trying to re-focus the debate, so that it is less about institutions and procedures and more about the delivery of appropriate policies for jobs, crime and the environment.

ASK YOURSELF

- How did the parties agree and differ in their approaches to Europe in the early post-war years?
- Why was Labour reluctant to support the first British application to join the EEC?
- Was Margaret Thatcher really anti-European?
- Why did Labour become markedly more pro-European after 1983?
- Are the differences between Labour and the Conservatives today more apparent than real?

91

MAIN TEXT

Labour

1945-1962

In the early years after 1945, when the European dream of a more closely united continent first appeared, Labour was sceptical of any moves in the direction of a unified Europe. Though a few individuals were well-disposed, the bulk of the party was unsympathetic to the rhetoric of Monnet and some of the other enthusiasts. They wanted nothing to do with integration, even though fellow-socialists on the other side of the Channel were much involved in the early moves. Attlee showed an insular approach, when he wrote in 1948: 'The Labour Party is a characteristically British production, differing widely from continental socialist parties. It is a product of its environment, and of the national habit of mind'. Europe was not a priority, and the Attlee Government thought in terms of Britain as a world power, with American and Commonwealth ties. His Foreign Secretary, Bevin, favoured a strong bond with America, and was keen to see US involvement in the defence of Europe, as in the NATO scheme; this was seen as more important than cooperation with Europe.

Labour disapproved of the supranationalistic implications of the ECSC, and was anyway in the process of nationalising the iron and steel industry. There seemed little point in taking over a 'commanding height of the economy' only to surrender control to Brussels, and so Britain played no part in the discussions concerned with setting up the body. Similarly, at the time of Britain's first attempt to enter the EEC, Harold Wilson, the Foreign Affairs spokesman, was unenthusiastic about membership: 'We are not entitled to sell our friends and kinsman down the river for a problematical and marginal advantage in selling washing-machines in Dusseldorf'. The mood of the 1962 Labour Conference was non-committal, and although the principle was left open there were conditions to be fulfilled before entry, notably important safeguards for the Commonwealth, and Commonwealth backing for the bid. The then leader, Gaitskell, was hostile, and spoke of the negotiations as marking 'the end of a thousand years of history'.

The Wilson years 1963-75

The party never displayed any real interest in joining what it portrayed as a 'rich man's club', and there was great scepticism about any benefits which might accrue. The Wilson Government toyed with the idea of closer EFTA and EEC links, and contemplated 'associate membership', but such thoughts never materialised. However, the leadership was aware of Britain's loss of world influence and economic decline, and gradually became convinced that there was no alternative to joining the EEC. With characteristic subtlety, he sold the idea to his party on the basis that his moves were only an attempt to discover the terms.

In early 1967, the Prime Minister and Foreign Secretary went on a tour of European capitals to see how much sympathy there was for British entry, but MPs and the party outside Westminster showed no marked fervour. Opposition was contained because some of its likely leaders were in the Cabinet, and so the abortive bid was made. It remained on the table after de Gaulle's veto.

In Opposition, after the 1970 election, Labour's underlying scepticism came to the surface. There was an element on the Right, associated particularly with Roy Jenkins, which was fervently pro-European; others in the party were either cool, or hostile, and as leader, Harold Wilson needed all of his skills to hold the party together. Faced with an almost unbridgeable gap, he compromised by saying that the terms were not right, and would need to be put to the people in a referendum.

After the election victories of 1974 and the successful conclusion of renegotiations, the Wilson Government commended the new terms to the electorate and suggested that Britain's best interests would be served by staying in the Community. He told the House that better terms had been conceded as a result of the discussions, and that in any case the EC was changing in ways that made it easier for Britain to adjust. The Labour Party as a whole was unconvinced. Many members still had deep reservations about the nature and development of the EC, and their deep reservations were voiced by some leading figures in the Cabinet. Ministers were allowed to 'agree to differ', but by 16-7 the Cabinet supported the recommendations.

When the clear result was announced, a leading 'anti', Tony Benn, accepted that his followers must abide by the verdict: 'I read the message loud and clear. When the British people speak, everyone - including ourselves - should tremble before their decisions'.

From Callaghan to Smith

In the late 1970s, under the Callaghan Government, ministers did not always behave as 'good Europeans' despite the outcome of the referendum, and some adopted a combative attitude in negotiations. The left-wing of the party remained uneasy about membership; they lamented a 'loss of sovereignty' and noted an accumulating trade deficit with other states. In Opposition, they became increasingly antagonistic, and the defection of some leading members of the Right to the Social Democrats strengthened their influence. In the 1983 election, Labour campaigned to withdraw from the Community, and lost heavily.

After Labour's humiliating defeat under the leadership of Michael Foot, there gradually began to emerge within the party a wider recognition that democratic socialists had a role to play in the development of the Community. The new Kinnock leadership gradually moved the party round to a more pro-European stance. He was by background and inclination a man of the Left, and as such had no liking for the EC. However, he soon came to understand that anti-Europeanism was one of a number of policies which helped to make Labour unelectable. He had never been as hostile as Tony Benn and others on the Left, so that some revisionism on Europe was not only desirable but feasible.

With the 1984 Euro-elections looming, an early modification in approach was essential. There was nothing dramatic, but he appeared open to persuasion. He indicated that it was necessary for the EEC to prove itself 'a source of tangible value to the British people' which involved 'no significant material loss or disadvantage'. His approach thereafter remained minimalist and pragmatic, a matter to be judged on the balance of economic advantage.

After Labour lost the 1987 election, policy towards Europe was re-assessed at the time of the *Policy Review*. He had by then come to acquire some admiration for European socialist leaders, of whom several were in office in charge of left-wing governments. They wanted to see Britain more committed to membership, and Neil Kinnock himself appreciated that having been in the Community for fifteen years there were difficulties and dangers which made it undesirable to leave. Moreover, Europe had begun to seriously divide the Conservative Government. There was possible party advantage to be gained in striking a more positive note.

Above all, however, it was the visit of Jacques Delors which was the catalyst for a change in Labour thinking. He spoke of the social dimension of the EC, and Labour found itself warming to the theme. After years in which many remnants of socialism were killed off under Margaret Thatcher, Labour realised that a version of it still survived on the continent. Via the Social Charter (as it was then known), there was a chance for the labour movement as a whole to reverse the tide. After this, there was a wider recognition that democratic socialists had a role to play in the development of the Community, and the Kinnock leadership wanted to play its part.

In 1989, Neil Kinnock fought the European elections on a manifesto commonly agreed by all the socialist parties in the Community, and Labour did well. By the end of the decade it had ceased to be an anti-European party, and was broadly at one with its associates in the EC; Labour MEPs were sitting with their fellows in the European Parliament. The leadership was committed to Britain playing an active role in Europe, and Labour often sounded markedly more positive than the Tory Government in its rhetoric. Its priorities were closely congruent with those which dominated the Community, and it was sniping at ministers over their negative approach.

By the early 1990s, it was not felt necessary to spell out a clear vision of the sort of Community Labour favoured, for it could sit back and watch the Conservatives get themselves involved in a damaging debate. Neil Kinnock explained the position thus:

We need a government in Britain that will participate in the development of Europe; that will play a direct, influential role in fashioning the institutions and relationships of the market in which our economy must work in order to prosper. Mrs Thatcher's failure to accept cooperation...is creating the threat of a two-tier Europe, with Britain firmly stuck in the second rank. We cannot afford that.

John Smith, the leader elected shortly after the election in 1992, had long been pro-European in his thinking, having supported entry in 1971-72. Though in favour of the Maastricht Bill and wanting to see it ratified, he faced a situation in which the Conservatives were in difficulty over the issue. Some of his colleagues were keen to see the Opposition exploit

Governmental weakness and unpopularity, and vote against ratification. Smith made the absence of the Social Chapter the focus of his attacks on ministers and his party abstained on other key votes - thus ensuring that the Bill proceeded.

By the early-mid 1990s, Labour seemed to be often criticising the Conservative Government for not being European enough, and suggested that Britain should play a more active role in developing European institutions and in making membership work to Britain's advantage. Its spokespersons poured scorn on John Major for refusing to sign up for the Social Chapter at Maastricht, and highlighted Tory divisions.

Tony Blair in opposition and office
Tony Blair was keen to sound positive on Europe, and in opposition was more sympathetic to the single currency and other Union plans than was the Major Government. It was relatively easy to sit back and watch Conservative MPs tear themselves apart on European policy. In office, charged with the responsibility for making fundamental decisions, he has inevitably been more constrained, but Labour appears to be moving towards adopting the Euro early in the new century, and has been keen to portray itself as a leading player in the EU (see also p56-59).

Labour past and present
Labour has had six broad positions on Europe since the war. Cool or hostile up until the late sixties, it moved to advocate entry in 1967, became lukewarm again in opposition after 1970, supported membership in the referendum, became sharply critical in the early 1980s and committed to membership later in the decade. This is how it portrays itself today. Labour is now in a broadly pro-European phase, committed to making membership work to Britain's advantage. Although before the 1997 election it was reluctant to commit itself too strongly, for fear of being portrayed by its principal opponents as meekly subservient to those who urged the cause of greater European integration, it has since its victory steered a generally positive course. It has signed the Social Chapter and pointed the way to eventual involvement in a single currency.

The Conservative Party

1945-57

In Opposition after the war, Winston Churchill's Zurich Speech and his involvement in organisations such as the 'United Europe Committee' combined to give the impression that he was sympathetic to political and economic union. Yet despite the language, his ideas were vague and he never seriously envisaged that Britain would be a member of a united Europe. As Prime Minister, he was dismissive of plans for a European Defence Community. His Government had no inclination to join such a body, and as with his successor, Eden, there was a reluctance to surrender national sovereignty to any European organisation. Europeans had been misled into thinking that Britain was a likely participant in their schemes for closer cooperation, whereas the British preferred to be friendly by-standers.

The Macmillan-Heath era, 1957-1975

Having rejected an invitation to participate in the Messina talks, Britain did not sign the Treaty of Rome in 1957. However, by 1960-1 the Macmillan Government had become convinced of the merits of joining the Community (see p29-30), but the attempt failed in 1963.

Conservative interest in the Community was heightened when Edward Heath became leader of the party in 1965, for he was committed to the European cause and saw the attempt to join as something of a crusade. When he gained the Premiership five years later, the circumstances were more propitious, and when he signed the Treaty of Accession in 1972 he saw it as an historic turning-point in Britain's fortunes. His Conservative successor never shared his degree of commitment.

1975-1997

Margaret Thatcher adopted a more mimimalist position. She could see the economic benefits of membership and wanted to see Britain stay in the Community. However, her outlook was more of a Gaullist one for she favoured a 'Europe des Patries'. For her, the EC was what she called in her Bruges Speech 'a partnership of nation-states each retaining the right to protect its vital interests more effectively than at present the habit of working together'.

To many members of the party, her approach was seen as determined - if sometimes strident - and there was some admiration for the way she defended her country's interests as she saw them. Party critics exhibited much irritation and resentment about her manner in dealing with European leaders, which could be carping and hectoring. Yet in spite of her strong stand for British interests, she was the one who, by signing the Single European Act, committed Britain to a path which she and others came to find increasingly distasteful. She favoured the idea of an internal market without controls in which businessmen could sell their wares without hindrance, but had no liking for any approach which involved a surrender of national sovereignty to the EC.

Ultimately, Mrs Thatcher's attitude towards Europe was her undoing, for the divisions within her party, more especially within her Government, proved difficult to contain. After 1986, several of her ministers left the Cabinet directly or indirectly because of policy towards the EC. For instance, in 1986 Michael Heseltine and Leon Brittan resigned over the 'Westland Affair', a dispute about whether the rescue of the helicopter firm should be by an American company or a European consortium. However, it was the resignation in 1990 of Sir Geoffrey Howe as Deputy Prime Minister which was the most damaging ministerial loss. He wanted Britain to join the ERM, and was increasingly alarmed by the shrillness of his leader's anti-European tone and her unwillingness to contemplate closer economic and political union. It was his departure which precipitated the leadership contest which led to her downfall.

John Major appeared to be a cool pragmatist on Europe. Soon after becoming leader, he made it clear that he wished to place Britain 'at the heart of Europe', but he was aware of the potential for division inherent in the issue. His immediate task was to keep the party together in the run-up to the 1992 election. He showed some skill in terms of party management, although pro-Europeans thought that this was at the expense of giving a clear lead to the country about the direction in which he wished to see the Community develop. Maastricht was a personal success, and his negotiation of a 'double opt-out' at first seemed to please many of his party followers. His critics would say that it was achieved on the basis of Britain being isolated from our European partners. But at least at that summit he did appear to make Britain an acceptable member of the European club once again.

After the 1992 election, with a small and ever-dwindling majority, he had a particularly difficult course to navigate. At the same time as he was trying to convince other members of the European Council that he was a 'good European', he was also concerned to assure his own right-wing that he was rolling back the influence of the EC. He courted the Euro-sceptics and the jingoistic vote in the country by a series of 'tough' stances towards our European partners, particularly over revised voting arrangements in the Council of Ministers and over the choice of a new President for the European Commission. In so doing, he sacrificed some support from pro-European Conservatives (particularly the more pro-federal MEPs) who were dismayed by his policy and approach post-Maastricht. Neither did he win the wholehearted backing of the Thatcherite Right - many of whom were prepared to back him in any successful stand he took, but who were never convinced that he was going far and fast enough in their chosen direction.

Mr Major was forced to give a high priority to questions of party unity. Like Harold Wilson in the Labour Party of the 1970s, he sought to perform a balancing act. He tried to be sceptical enough to win round the wavering Thatcherites, and constructive enough to keep pro-Europeans content. The attempt was not a success, and he ended up pleasing very few of his nominal supporters. Europe proved a seriously damaging issue in the run-up to the 1997 election.

1997 and subsequently

William Hague has adopted a cool tone towards Europe and especially towards the single currency which he does not think that Britain should join in this or the next Parliament. His position was in some respects reinforced by the outcome of a party ballot (October 1998) on British participation in the Euro. He appealed over the heads of the divided Parliamentary Party to win overwhelming grassroots support for his determination to fight the next election on an anti-EMU ticket. In a 58.9% turnout, 84.4% backed his hard-line European stance, but hopes that it would end the civil war within he party have proved to be misplaced. The leader - using an old Texan phrase - dismisses the big pro-European guns who oppose him as 'big hats and no cattle'. Pro-Europeans have generally felt dismayed at his tone. They did not approve of the holding of the vote which they saw as needlessly divisive. They accused him of splitting the party, alienating business and of losing the vital centre ground on which elections are won. In their view, the result of any consultation in which people were asked to support the leadership position was meaningless, a foregone conclusion given the party tradition of loyalty.

The issue was potentially divisive when the party came to devise its manifesto for the 1999 Euro-elections. Yet in the event, the divisions did not erupt as seriously as they might have done. There was a breakaway movement, the Pro-European Conservatives, but it failed to attract support from key Euro-philes such as Kenneth Clarke and Michael Heseltine. They agreed to 'keep quiet' in the campaign, feeling that they could find living space under the party umbrella - based as it was on the slogan: 'In Europe, but not run by Europe'. Most other Conservatives were pleased to see membership of the Euro ruled out for this Parliament or the next.

As the year progressed, the delicate nature of the party's balancing act came under increasing pressure. Pro-Europeans saw the leadership as moving further to the Right and feared that the voices of those who doubted whether Britain should even be in the Union were being listened to with excessive respect.

The speeches of leading figures at the Blackpool Conference (October 1999) indicated just how far the party had shifted its position. Shadow Foreign Secretary John Maples promised to 'stop the slide to a European super-state' by making it a priority to amend the Treaty of Rome so as to allow member states to opt out of laws they do not wish to implement. The leader demanded a flexibility clause in any new EU treaty, 'or else ... there will be no new treaty'.

For the likes of Kenneth Clarke, the mood at Blackpool was profoundly discouraging. As he put it: 'This kind of extremism is quite contrary to the tradition of Tory internationalism'. He was dismissive of any amendment to the Treaty of Rome which in his view was neither practical nor necessary, and offered to help Mr Hague fend of Euro-sceptic pressure to make Conservative policy even more 'extreme, anti-European and revengeful' - an offer not taken up.

Overall, William Hague has planted his feet firmly on the high ground of Euro-scepticism. He is a deep-seated anti-federalist, and believes[1] that integrationist solutions for Europe's future are the answers of the past. He sees European leaders as men applying '1950s solutions for the problems of the 1940s', and suggests that old men's answers are inappropriate for the millennium: 'The post-war consensus in favour of economic, strategic and political integration in Europe is outdated in a globalised high-tech world, along with the interventionist 'big state' corporatist mindset which accompanies it...Some say European political integration is inevitable and that Britain must jump on board or miss the boat. I say to them that it is not inevitable'.

Europe has consumed the Tory Party for several years. It made life near impossible for John Major, as he tried to strike a middle way between two irreconcilable sides. William Hague is likely to find that his tougher stance still gets a rough ride. Leaders seem to be damned when they do not proclaim distinctive policies and damned when they do. If they give a clear lead, there is the danger of losing the support of a particular wing of the party. If they fail to provide such a lead, then others take control and set the party agenda. A referendum could still be some years away, and until it is held the fratricide is likely to continue.

Past and present

At present, a very fragile unity has been achieved within the Conservative Party, on the basis that the majority of the party take a Hagueish viewpoint or one even more hostile to the single currency. But in late 1999 it is still possible to identify a number of different positions on European questions. The Heath approach is pro-federalist, and he believes that moves towards a 'United States of Europe' are clearly to be welcomed, 'the quicker the better'. Though he has not sought to cultivate a band of followers for his vision, there is a small grouping within the parliamentary party which shares much of his thinking. Unashamed pro-Europeans include Kenneth Clarke and Michael Heseltine.

Michael Portillo, and some others on the Right, disapprove of many aspects of the Union, whilst accepting the economic benefits of membership. They abhor the Heathite 'nightmare', and would prefer to see the EU develop as a looser entity to which Britain does not have to yield any further sovereignty. The ultra-sceptic Norman Lamont has questioned the value of British membership. Along with some other Tories, he is unconvinced that it has produced many beneficial results, even if as yet he has not campaigned for withdrawal. As he put it to the Tory Conference: 'I do not suggest Britain should today unilaterally withdraw from Europe. But the issue may well return to the political agenda'.

In between are the bulk of the party who do not wish to see any further steps towards integration. They dislike any federal notions and disapprove of the 'social Europe' originally associated with Jacques Delors. Most members are Thatcherite in tone. They favour a single market, but are very hostile to any move to greater political unity. They prefer a 'Europe de Patries', along Gaullist lines.

A summary of attitudes in the Parliamentary Party

The Leadership
Most closet Europeans in the last Cabinet have disappeared, although Sir George Young is sympathetic to the notion of a single currency. The Shadow Cabinet is anti-federalist, and the whole tone of the Hague team is increasingly Euro-sceptical.

The MPs
A majority follow the leadership, and are cool on Europe. They recognise the damage done by division, and wish to play the issue down as much as possible. However, increasingly the tone of debate leans to the right-wing position (Euro-agnostics veering to Euro-scepticism).

The Right contains some MPs who are anti-Europeans, opposed on principle to membership of the European Union, usually but not always on constitutional grounds. It also includes a large number of hardened Euro-sceptics, who support membership in order to achieve a single market but are opposed to moves to achieve anything beyond that.

A smaller pro-European element (Euro-enthusiasts) comes mainly from the left of the party, and in the face of adversity it has been forced to become better organised. The Tory Reform Group, the Conservative Group for Europe and the Action centre for Europe have joined forces under the umbrella of Conservative Mainstream, bringing together leading members of past Tory Cabinets such as Messrs Clarke, Gummer and Heseltine.

The Conservatives have a habit of enthusiastically embracing Europe followed by pangs of guilt as they wonder whether it was such a good idea after all. Mr Heath took Britain into Europe in the first place and has never quite been forgiven by many for realising his dream. Margaret Thatcher pushed forward the Single European Act, and then spent the rest of her Premiership railing against some of its effects. John Major signed the Maastricht Treaty which set the framework for the single currency, and was then crippled by a Tory European civil war - despite negotiating an opt-out clause.

The Liberals/Alliance/Liberal Democrats

The Liberals supported closer integration and British participation in it long before the two main parties were prepared to take this route. Inevitably, theirs' was a minority voice, and the absence of coalition politics at Westminster meant that it was rarely advanced at the top table. They supported the attempts to join the EC made by the Macmillan and Wilson Governments. Later, they gave solid backing to Edward Heath in the debates over accession in the early 1970s and joined him on the pro-European side in the Referendum campaign.

Some right-wing members of the Labour Party broke away from their past allegiance in 1981 to form the Social Democratic Party. Pro-Europeanism was one of their most distinctive policies, and - led initially by Roy Jenkins, a former President of the European Commission - they campaigned with the Liberals as the Alliance in 1983. They strongly condemned Labour's support for withdrawal. When the Alliance evolved into the merged Liberal Democrat Party, Paddy Ashdown kept alive the traditional Centre support for European cooperation. The bulk of the party has retained a pro-federalist line, though there are individuals who are uneasy about the commitment to political unity exhibited by the leadership.

For a long while the pro-European third party has been hampered in its political progress by the First Past The Post electoral system which has operated in Westminster and European elections. In spite of this, the Liberal Democrats managed to win their first two seats in the European Parliament in 1994. They then scored impressively in the 1997 election, winning 46 seats, and then worked with the new Labour Administration to bring about a change in the method of voting in time for the 1999 Euro-elections (see p67-68).

British parties and the 1999 European Elections: key policies

	Labour	Conservative	Liberal Democrat
Budget	Proud to have secured Britain's rebate; package agreed at Berlin summit imposes no further burdens on tax payer.	Wish to reduce EU budget, and the British net contribution to the Union.	Oppose any rise in UK contribution, and wish to retain rebate.
Defence	Not mentioned in Labour document but PES[1] want closer co-operation in foreign policy and an enhanced defence capacity.	Disapproval of a European defence identity outside of NATO. No European army.	Greater co-operation wanted to allow national forces to operate alongside each other.
Enlargement	Favour enlargement as '... right in itself ... has the potential to make Europe the largest, most competitive single market in the world'.	Pro-enlargement; a priority which would advance free markets and free trade.	Keen. Would be a means of uniting Europe on the basis of economic and political freedom.
Fraud	Reform needed to embrace overhaul of machinery for awarding contracts, financial accountability and disciplinary proceedings for Commission staff.	Want an independent anti-fraud office outside the European Commission; also tougher powers for Parliament and new codes of conduct.	Need a strengthened anti-fraud unit which can impose swinging penalties; fraud should be cut following reform of CAP[2].
Home affairs	Not mentioned, but PES keen to strengthen law enforcement co-operation and improve democratic accountability of Europol.	Strong disapproval of Europe-wide criminal justice system: 'no' to a common immigration system.	Support Europol and favour its expansion - but with adequate checks for civil liberties.
Reform	Want new structure for Commission and improved decision-making/account-ability.	Other than re single market, want more freedom for national governments to choose which EU policies to adopt. No erosion of British veto.	More QMV[3] in an enlarged Union. Also, a need for an EU constitution to define Union powers.
Single currency	Keen to join a successful currency, subject to economic circumstances.	British participation ruled out for this and next Parliament.	Keen to join as soon as possible; want an early referendum.

1	PES	Party of European Socialists
2	CAP	Common Agricultural Policy
3	QMV	Qualified Majority Voting

NB The three main parties put up candidates for all 84 mainland seats, as did the Pro-Euro Conservative Party, the UK Independence Party, the Greens and the Natural Law Party. Plaid Cymru contested all five Welsh vacancies, the SNP all eight Scottish ones.

The impact of the European issue on the parties

In no other country have the parties and politicians found the European issue so difficult to handle. Just as Home Rule for Ireland was a divisive question in the 1880s, and Tariff Reform was in the first decade of the C20, so Europe has been in post-war years. The issue of integration has divided both parties for more than forty years, ever since the Attlee Government declined to take part in the negotiations leading to the Treaty of Paris and the creation of the ECSC.

What has been remarkable about the splits within each party is not so much their longevity but rather their intensity. At various times, Europe has constituted the fault line within each party, offering the prospect of splitting it asunder. As they have had to contend with these internal divisions, the temptation for party leaders has been to adopt short-term policies which have got them off the hook until the next election was safely out of the way.

This was true of the Labour Party in the 1970s, yet whatever reluctance it showed in Opposition the leadership generally came to agree with the Conservatives that Britain's place was in the Community as soon as it regained power. In recent years, it has retained that more positive approach, and Labour has now outflanked the Conservatives as the more pro-European party.

The Conservatives have found themselves preoccupied with matters of unity more recently, and have had to minimise the extent of the commitments they have undertaken in order to hold the party together. For John Major, the task was the more difficult as his predecessor was playing the nationalist card with some bravura. If Labour's disunity was over the actual fact of membership, the issue for the Conservatives has been different. Few felt that Britain could survive outside the Community/Union, but many were uncertain as to the sort of future they wanted inside it. Most politicians and writers agree that there is little to be gained from espousing an anti-European viewpoint today; the debate has moved on, and there is no going back. All three parties are officially in favour of 'Britain in Europe'.

Indeed, the differences between them are considerable, but not fundamental. The Liberal Democrats are most committed, and see the merits of a more federal structure, though some worry about parading this viewpoint too often in public. Labour has seen an advantage in keeping a step ahead of the Conservative Party, though its past record invites some misgivings about the depth of its conversion. In office, it has shown a willingness to 'make Europe work for Britain', whilst not capitulating to every demand made by other European leaders and the Commission in Brussels. In its rhetoric it is more enthusiastic about meeting the conditions of convergence which makes a single currency viable, and it was happy to embrace the Social Chapter. Yet it too still shies away from the word 'federal', and like the previous Conservative Government is wary about any moves to deeper integration.

CONCLUSION

European policy has been hotly contested by the main parties and within them. On certain recent issues such as the Social Chapter, the issue has resolved itself into a straight Left-Right disagreement, with present ministers keen to sign the document soon after assuming power. Yet on British participation in the single currency there are differing views in both parties, with the Conservatives exhibiting the sharpest and most public divisions. As Simon Bulmer has pointed out[2]: 'It is this mixture of divisions between and within the two main parties that has characterised the European 'fault-line' in British party politics'.

Pressure groups and popular opinion

INTRODUCTION

Since 1973, the British people and organisations representing them have had to adjust to a world in which many of the policies which concern them are decided not in Whitehall/Westminster but in Brussels. This has been particularly true since the passage of the Single European Act and the signing of the Maastricht Treaty. Whether or not they are pro-European in their thinking, individuals and groups have to accept that Europe plays an increasing part in our lives and that policy-making now has an important European dimension.

ASK YOURSELF

- Why have British pressure groups found it worthwhile to lobby so extensively in Brussels and Strasbourg?
- In what ways might a major group such as the Confederation of British Industry seek to influence European initiatives?
- What are the disadvantages and benefits to be obtained from employing a professional lobbying company?
- Why have the British people had such an ambivalent approach to the European Community/Union since 1973?
- Do you see yourself as a European citizen or as a British one? Why?

MAIN TEXT

Pressure groups and Europe

Many British pressure groups have lobbied the European Community/Union
in recent years. Indeed, Grant has estimated[1] that the number of employees
of such groups engaged on work in Brussels doubled to more than 10,000
between the late 1980s and the mid 1990s. The increase indicates the
growth in importance which pressure groups have attached to Europe,
particularly as the pace of development towards greater integration
intensified with the signing of the Single European Act and then the
Maastricht Treaty.

Many decisions are now taken in Brussels, including those in areas of
growing importance such as animal welfare and the environment, as well as
on subjects such as agriculture in which the European Commission has long
been involved. Since the passage of the SEA, more of these decisions have
been taken on the basis of majority voting, and this has meant that groups
have needed to be more sophisticated in choosing their targets to approach.

In the last few years, there has been a marked growth in professional
lobbying at the EU level. For a substantial fee, lobbying firms will monitor
developments in particular areas of policy, and suggest possible contacts,
arrange meetings and generally help groups which themselves may lack the
right connections to put over a powerful case. Many firms and groups
combine their own lobbying with the use of professional agencies.

Pressure groups and access to the EU

There are three different routes by which pressure groups can lobby the
European Union. They may:

- put pressure on the British Government, hoping to encourage it to take a
  strong line in negotiations in the Council of Ministers
- become part of a Euro-group, one of the federations of like-minded groups
  which operate across the Union
- lobby the institutions of the Union directly, by approaching the European
  Commission (maybe even a Commissioner), the Parliament or one of its
  committees (by approaching their MEP or acting with a group of MEPs),

the Court of Justice or even on occasion national representatives in the Council of Ministers before it meets. They may maintain an office in Brussels to give them easier access, and enable them to sustain a closer monitoring of thinking and developments in the Union.

Some government departments in Whitehall are much concerned in matters European. The Foreign Office and the Treasury are obvious examples, but the Departments of Agriculture and Trade are also very relevant. Pressure groups operating in these areas will often choose to make contact with departmental officials. For instance, representatives of the National Farmers Union finds it helpful to meet senior civil servants to urge ministers to assert British interests in the Council of Ministers. This was true in the beef crisis, but also over many aspects of the working of the Common Agricultural Policy.

Usually, the Commission is the prime target, and as a relatively open bureaucracy it welcomes approaches from interested parties. It maintains a list of several hundred bodies whose spokespersons it automatically consults on matters relating to technical legislation. In particular, it has dealings with several Euro-groups which are favoured because they represent a wide span of opinion. Such Euro and other groups have begun to attach more importance to the European Parliament in recent years, for its influence and legislative powers have increased considerably as a result of recent treaties. The Court too, is of growing significance. British environmental groups lobbied its members in connection with the quality of drinking water, and on matters such as pit closures and legal aid it has been approached.

As we have seen, some groups use a number of different avenues when lobbying Europe. They may use a professional agency, tackle their own national officials and ministers, and also adopt a Brussels/Strasbourg/ Luxembourg strategy.

British groups operating at the European level and the routes they find most useful

The British groups which are most involved with the Union are business/trade organisations, and those representing trade unionists, farmers and environmentalists, including those specialising in matters of animal welfare. In his survey of 100 or so business, labour and cause groups, Baggott found[2] that 12% of them had offices based in Europe, but more than

75% had become a member of a European-wide pressure group, defending their cause or interest at this level. The business groups had been especially active in employing both strategies.

Among the business groups, the Institute of Directors is much involved in watching EU developments. It is an umbrella group which defends the interests of 'big business', as represented by its 38,000 members. Pro-free market policies and wary of the Social Chapter, the single currency and other integrationist tendencies, it nonetheless recognises that membership of the Union has a considerable impact on issues of concern to its members, affecting British trade and manufacturing. Much legislation affecting companies now originates in Brussels. Accordingly, it lobbies via its office there, and through UNICE (see box opposite), the Euro-group for manufacturers. It sees the Commission as its prime target, although it also seeks to win the support of groups of MEPs and Parliament's committees.

Trade unionists discovered the value of the Community as an outlet for their campaigning rather later than manufacturing organisations such as the CBI. It was the visit of Jacques Delors to the TUC Conference (1988) which had made the TUC realise the possibilities of achieving valuable protective legislation via the Social Chapter. But some individual unions were finding - especially after the signing of the SEA, with its move towards the creation of a single market - that they had an important interest in decisions taken in Brussels. Often their own members might work in the Community (more the case with professions), or find themselves travelling across the continent - e.g., T&GWU members who worked as long-distance lorry drivers.

Of the environmental groups, Greenpeace operates on an international basis, and its various national organisations have put pressure on the Commission and Parliament. Friends of the Earth attaches importance to these outlets, often finding that they can provide a more sympathetic hearing than that given by British governments over the last two decades.

Among the professional groups, the British Medical Association and the Law Society are two of the groups most actively engaged at the EU level. The BMA has committees specialising in European-wide issues and lobbies the Commission directly, as well as indirectly via British ministers. The Law Society, since the passage of the SEA, has lawyers who belong to it working in the Union. To protect their interests, it has a base in Brussels.

THE VOICE OF EUROPEAN BUSINESS AND INDUSTRY

UNICE's priorities are

- improvement of European competitiveness leading to growth and to creation of lasting jobs
- completion of all aspects of the Single Market
- progress towards Economic and Monetary Union with a European System of Central Banks and a single currency
- pursuit of economic and social cohesion in the EU
- development of social policies compatible with the need for competitiveness and economic growth
- support for the restructuring and economic development of central and eastern European countries
- liberalisation of world trade
- promotion of European technology, research and development
- protection of the environment based on sustainable development

UNICE is a Euro-group, a federation of national pro-business interest groups

UNICE is

- the official voice of European business and industry vis-a-vis the EU institutions; it was established in 1958
- composed of 33 central industry and employers' federations from 25 European countries, with a permanent Secretariat based in Brussels.

UNICE's purpose is

- to keep abreast of issues that interest its members by maintaining permanent contacts with all the European institutions
- to provide a framework which enables industry and employers to examine European policies and proposed legislation, and to prepare joint positions
- to promote its policies and positions at Community and national level, and persuade the European legislators to take them into account
- to represent its members in the dialogue between social partners provided for in the treaty on EU.

Public opinion and the EU

From the time when Britain first had dealings with the European Community, the public has often seemed ill-informed and confused about Europe. Euro-sceptics have been able to point to popular misgivings about Europe in order to substantiate their case against closer integration. Pro-Europeans argue that the case for Europe is rarely put to the country, because governments have been reluctant to 'sell' the European idea or the advantages gained from membership; what the public do get is regular Euro-bashing from sections of the tabloid press which are keen to point to the disadvantages of life in the Union.

When the public was directly consulted by the Labour Government on continued membership in 1975, it gave an overwhelming response in favour, by approximately 2:1. On that occasion, politicians did address the country, arguing the case against withdrawal and explaining what might be gained by 'staying in' the Community. When Labour committed itself to withdrawal from the EC in the early 1980s, there was little sign that its anti-Community rhetoric was electorally a bonus. Indeed throughout the decade *Eurobarometer*, the EC's polling organisation, found that the majority of British respondents favoured European unification in some form.

Over the last decade or so, there has been more evidence of what membership means for Britain, as the impact of some EC policies has become more apparent. Moreover, since the passage of the Single European Act there has been a developing momentum within the Community/Union to drive the process of integration forward. Britain has been faced with more policies which some politicians and people find unpalatable, ranging from border controls to the single currency, from the fisheries policy to tax harmonisation. Against this background, the public mood seems to be broadly in favour of the European enterprise, but without enthusiasm for closer integration. The British are not alone in this drift of opinion, for the Danes also are markedly less sympathetic to integration than are some of the other continental countries.

Public opinion has been sensitive to the attitudes adopted by political leaders and the media, and also to the turn of events. For instance, in 1974, a year after Britain joined the EC, a 3:2 majority favoured withdrawal. Yet a year later, the tide had turned sharply in the run-up to the Referendum.

Recent polling evidence

Poll findings echo much of the ambiguity over Europe to which we have referred. An ICM poll for *The Observer (December 1998)*, suggested that there was a 3:2 majority against Britain joining a single currency, although when asked whether Britain could afford to stay out if the currency proved to be a success there was agreement by 2:1 that we could not. If the Euro fails, there will be no referendum. Only if it succeeds, will voters be called on to make a decision. Under these circumstances, the Government, much of industry and several of the unions would probably campaign for a 'Yes' vote, and in this situation there is a strong likelihood that public opinion would be transformed and that Britain would decide to join by a substantial majority.

The same poll showed that readers of the *Mail, Sun, Telegraph* and *Times* which all take a Euro-sceptic line agree by 53% to 36% that Britain could not afford to stay out of a successful Euro. The editors of these papers may need to re-think their line on Europe if the currency works well. Significantly, when asked how much they trusted their daily newspaper to tell the truth about European issues 25% of all respondents were prepared to offer their trust, 52% had little trust and 18% no trust at all!

The poll showed little enthusiasm for tax harmonisation on which the tabloids have made great play, and only 30% backed ministers in their stance of co-operating with the rest of the Union, where this 'makes sense'. 55% felt that 'all decisions on tax should be decided in Britain and not involve Europe at all'.

Earlier in 1998 (March), a *Eurobarometer* poll was quoted in *The Guardian*. It dealt with support for the EU across the Union, asking whether it was a 'Good Thing' or a 'Bad Thing'. The greatest support came from Ireland (83%), followed closely by the Netherlands and Luxembourg. Italy, Greece, Portugal and Spain also revealed a massive majority in favour. Significantly, many of these countries have done well out of the Union, either getting more out than they put in, or else being small states whose influence is proportionately greater within the organisation than it would be outside. The average scores were 49% in favour, 14% against. Britain ranked 13th out of 15, with 36% feeling that membership was a 'Good Thing', 23% a 'Bad Thing'. Only respondents in Austria and Sweden showed less enthusiasm.

CONCLUSION

The public mood is seemingly ambivalent, accepting that Britain's future must lie in Europe if we are not to be left out in the cold, but having deep reservations about the extent of the commitment. Many voters still do not feel truly European, in the way that some continentals might do.

Meanwhile, those who represent the public - parties and pressure groups - have had to adapt to Britain's membership or be left behind. Groups lobby those who exercise power, and well before the public became aware of the implications of membership agricultural and business interests were actively engaging with the European Community as it then was.

Some EU policies and their impact on Britain

INTRODUCTION

In the Treaty of Rome, there is reference to three 'common' policy areas, agriculture, commerce and transport. The emphasis was upon the development of a common market without trading barriers, and this remains an important feature of the Union. However, in recent years the EU has become more than a Common Market, as cooperation has been extended into other areas of policy. Some of these are economic, but others cover such areas as combating crime, immigration and foreign and security policy.

The trend has been for Brussels to become more involved in the life of its citizens, a situation which many European citizens appear to welcome. Eurobarometer findings suggest that many European people like to see Europe-wide decision-making on matters where the problems cross frontiers - e.g., the environment and overseas aid - but prefer national action on issues which more directly impact upon their existence - e.g., education and health.

ASK YOURSELF

- Why are there common policies on some others but not on others?
- What sort of issues should be handled at the EU level?
- Why is further reform of the Common Agricultural Policy necessary?
- What benefits are there for Britain in joining a single currency?
- Is it desirable that Europe should develop a stronger Common Foreign and Security Policy? Why has this been difficult to achieve?

MAIN TEXT

The picture of European Union involvement in policy-making is a patchy one, with strong involvement in some areas such as agriculture and fishing, joint policy-making between national governments and the EU in environmental and regional matters, and much less or no involvement in housing and welfare policy.

The range of policies undertaken by the Union is now extensive, including some where in the past there was little direction from Brussels. This is especially true of those matters concerning the environment, and those which form the second and third pillars of the Maastricht Treaty - the common foreign and security policy, and justice and home affairs.

The effectiveness of Union action varies according to the issue, and Nugent[1] has suggested that three key factors determine the pace and manner of advance:

i. The leadership given by the Commission
ii. The perceptions of the member states of what is desirable
iii.The individual and collective capacities of the member states to translate their perceptions into practice.

In the rest of this chapter, we have space to consider a limited range of EU policies, with particular reference to the way in which they affect Britain.

Agriculture: Common Agricultural Policy (CAP)

The origins of the CAP date back to the early days of the EEC. The Treaty of Rome set out the main objectives of agricultural policy, as being:

* to increase agricultural productivity
* to ensure a fair standard of living for the agricultural community
* to stabilise markets and to ensure that supplies are available to the consumer at reasonable prices.

The policy was finalised in 1962, after intense discussion between the French and German representatives. It was designed to protect rural interests in Europe, and at the same time provide industry with the prospect of a customs union of goods, services and capital. The French wanted guaranteed markets and prices for their farmers' agricultural produce, and the Germans wanted a wider market for their manufactured goods.

When the policy was established, agriculture was a key element in the economies of several states. In France, the farmers formed a significant section of the electorate; no French government could afford to alienate the agrarian lobby. In Germany too, the farmers were an important bloc, and at the time of the creation of the CAP it had the most protected agriculture among The Six. The policy was devised with the interests of such farmers in mind, and indeed the language of the objectives set out in Article 39 of the Rome Treaty bears a striking resemblance to that of the German Agricultural Act of 1955, with its talk of increased production to provide a reasonable standard of life for the farming community.

At first the policy had many attractions. The background was that people on the continent had been accustomed to shortages, and in the early post-war years there was much hunger and even near-starvation in some countries. Hence there was an emphasis on devising a policy which was able to provide plentiful food at reasonable prices. The CAP appeared to solve the problem of insufficient output, and also gave farmers a reasonable return for their endeavours, whilst keeping prices to the consumer under control.

Without the CAP there would probably have been no Community, for the memories of wartime shortages and the problems faced by farmers were much in the mind of many continental players. But times have moved on, and although agriculture is still highly significant in the EU economy its role is markedly less important than that of manufacturing industry and services. The number of farms has declined in all member states, some of the original Six having lost almost half or even more since the policy began. Belgium has declined from 184,000 to around 76,000 since 1970, Germany from 1,075,000 to around 606,000, and the Netherlands from 185,000 to around 120,000. Whereas in 1958 some 20% of EC employment was concerned with agricultural tasks, today the figure has fallen to around 5%.

By the early 1980s, farming had become much more efficient, partly as a result of technical progress but also because farmers had been encouraged to produce high quantities in the knowledge that they had guaranteed prices for their output. There were shortages no longer, and indeed the reverse was true. Huge quantities of unwanted products were being produced, so that

117
● ● ●

there were 'butter mountains' and 'milk and wine lakes'. This meant that European taxpayers were paying twice, partly by way of subsidies to the farmers and secondly because of the need to store unwanted goods. The sale of cut-price butter to the Russians did nothing for the credibility of the CAP.

It was essential to find some means of reducing the cost of agriculture to the Community, for it was absorbing a huge proportion of the Budget, 80.6% in 1973 when Britain joined the Community and still 67% in 1989 by which time discussion of the need for change was underway. Fundamental reform was essential, and the Commission had to find ways of bringing supply and demand into better balance. The days of open-ended price support were coming to an end, and it was a major goal of any reform to cut back production and compensate farmers for any loss of income.

The MacSharry Reforms agreed in 1992 were designed to reduce production, and thereby bring supply more into line with demand. Farmers were encouraged to produce less intensively, to diversify away from surplus products and to take early retirement.

The centrepiece of the changes was to move towards a system of direct income support rather than a reliance on price support, so that there were complicated schemes to compensate farmers for their loss of income. Specifically, there was a sharp reduction in prices paid to farmer (of nearly 30% for wheat and 15% for beef), a percentage of land was to be 'set-aside', and there was to be direct compensation (grants) to farmers to compensate for their loss of income. There were also schemes to encourage them to take early retirement.

The CAP was half-reformed in 1992, and the measures were taken further three years later as the EU tried to adapt its farm regime to the new GATT world trade system. The Americans and others had insisted that the EU phase out its price-support approach, which amounted to a massive subsidy to the exports of the EU's excess crops. In a sense, this has worked, and the grain and beef mountains and wine lakes have dwindled away.

At the Berlin summit in March 1999, further changes in agricultural policy were announced, although they were of a modest nature. In return for allowing Britain to retain its budget rebate, the French demanded concessions on agricultural policy. Some of the planned cuts in beef and cereal prices were restored and amendments to the dairy regime were staved off for another five years. 'Delay and dilute' was the French negotiating tactic, and even the cap on farm spending of £30b a year (nearly half the EU budget) may be difficult to achieve in the light of the French assault on reform plans. The aim was to re-direct the budget away from guaranteed prices for farmers towards direct income subsidy for those in need.

Under such reforms, the CAP is progressively shifting its farm subsidies away from price protection (which keeps the costs of EU groceries so high) and the storage of surpluses to subsidising the incomes of individual farmers via direct payments. (This is partly intended to help keep the marginal and hill farmers on the land of which they are the main custodians). This means that price support payments will continue to fall, at a rate of about 20% by 2000 for cereals and even more sharply for beef.

The trend to reform is set to continue, for if and when enlargement goes ahead, it is widely recognised that agricultural spending in existing countries will need to be controlled, not least because in states such as Poland some one in four workers still labour on the land and the Czechs, Hungarians and others have large agricultural sectors. The cost of extending the CAP in its present form would be prohibitive. Furthermore, there are constant demands for spending in sectors other than agriculture. Recent EU budgets have seen a decline in spending on agriculture which now consumes less than 50% of total expenditure (40.8b ecu out of 82.4billion).

Although the package of the early 1990s was a step in the direction of reform, more action is needed. The election in late 1998 of a German Government less dependent on the agrarian vote may facilitate the process; the Schroder Administration believes that the cost of the CAP could be eased if farm subsidies were to be reformed.

Britain and the CAP

Britain had traditionally pursued a 'cheap food' policy before joining the EC, and on this side of the Channel there was much denigration of the CAP which was seen as keeping prices unnecessarily high. Farmers who stood to benefit from it had little complaint, but from an early stage of membership politicians railed against a system which they claimed meant that Britain was paying an excessively large sum into the Community budget, money which was largely being spent on subsidising inefficient French farmers. The

A crisis in British agriculture?

Farm incomes were at a near peak in the early 1990s, but since then British farmers have experienced a difficult period, and farmers seem likely to face further difficulties. A crisis of confidence caused by BSE and other food scares has been made worse because of the strength of the pound which has hit all types of farming. Under the CAP, minimum prices for animals and crops have been set in euros, and so as the pound has risen the value of agricultural products has fallen - for instance, thereby making Irish beef cheaper than its British equivalent. Farm incomes have dropped by almost half according to NFU figures, and in Scotland and Wales hill farmers are lucky to make £10,000 a year.

Moreover, the situation is unlikely to improve, for as enlargement of the Union comes about price-support payments will continue to drop, and the share of the farm subsidies received by current EU members is likely to fall.

One door closes, another opens (for some)

Reports suggest[2] that the prospect of hard times ahead is encouraging some farmers as well as City businessmen to join the rush to acquire cheap land in Central and Eastern European countries which are lining up to join the European Union. Best fertile land in Hungary and Poland sells for about a tenth of the price it commands in East Anglia, and elsewhere in the Czech Republic, Estonia and Slovenia there is plenty of cheap land available. As some countries are reluctant to sell land, an alternative is rental, which is also very cheap. In most cases the land is rented on a long lease, with the option to buy at a distant date.

For all of the talk about CAP reform, it is unlikely to be quickly achieved, and investors are hoping to benefit from the same subsidies as farmers throughout the Union can currently obtain. Such farming is likely to be highly profitable by virtue of the payments available, even without allowing for the sale of crops produced. Western-style management and distribution techniques should help to further boost profit ratios.

Austrian, Dutch and German landowners are also cashing in on the trend, lured by the possibility of handsome gains. Environmentalists are less happy, for they fear that damage will be done to the rich variety of wildlife which thrives on what were inefficient collective farms. Birds that are rare in Britain still abound in Central Europe, and Poland has brown bears, lynxes, wolves and re-introduced bison roaming its forests.

attack has been maintained ever since, for in the 1990s the cost of the CAP are still roundly condemned. Critics claim that food could be purchased on the world market more cheaply than via the CAP, and they deride the alleged benefits of stability of supply which the policy offers.

Inevitably, Britain was going to benefit less from the CAP than some other countries. The policy was devised largely in their interests. Britain has always had a much smaller agricultural sector than France and Germany, and it has been a relatively efficient industry which needed the protection of guaranteed prices less than they did.

Overall, the era of British membership of the European Community/Union has been good for farming. There has been high productivity - partly because farmers own some of the Union's largest farms - and the country has become self-sufficient in produce such as cereals. Farmers have benefited from the substantial subsidies paid to them, and those who farmed intensively on large stretches of land have also received heavy set-aside payments. Yet farm incomes have fluctuated considerably, and have overall fallen in real terms since 1973 for two reasons (see box opposite):

- Production costs in Britain have been the highest in the EU even before the recent rise in the pound, perhaps a feature of high interest rates
- World prices of agricultural products have fallen in real terms over the last decade or more, especially in cereals and livestock which are a key element of British agriculture.

The main British parties favour further reform of a policy seen to be wasteful and inefficient. Many members on all sides of the House claim that it represents a bad deal for consumers and taxpayers. Labour supports fundamental change, but recognises the difficulty in achieving it. The Right of the Conservative Party is particularly antagonistic to the CAP and dislike its interventionist tone; they would prefer to see a more market-oriented approach to agriculture.

Economic and Monetary Union (EMU): the single currency

Economic and Monetary Union was not mentioned in any of the Treaties until the Single European Act of 1986, although the goal of EMU had been set out at a meeting of the heads of government at The Hague, back in 1969. The first modern plan for a single currency was proposed by the then Prime Minister of Luxembourg back in 1970, but hopes were scuppered by the oil crisis of 1973-1974. The idea was taken up by Jacques Delors, and in 1988 work began on what became known as the Delors Report, which in turn led to the decision to convene an Intergovernmental Conference (IGC) to debate this and other issues. The outcome of the IGC was the Maastricht Treaty.

At Maastricht, preparations were made to move towards economic and monetary union. A timetable was laid out, and convergence criteria (see p124) established by which a nation's suitability for entry would be judged. In 1998, it was agreed that 11 nations were ready for entry, and Britain - which had secured an 'opt-out' at Maastricht - decided not to be in the first wave of entrants. Denmark and Sweden also decided against entry, and Greece - which wanted to join - was declared unready.

With EMU achieved, the currencies of the member states are irrevocably locked to one another at the same exchange rate. Devaluations and revaluations of individual currencies are a thing of the past. The Euro will become in time the currency for use in all transactions, for after 2002 other notes and coins are due to disappear. From day one, the European Central Bank set a single interest rate for the entire euro-zone, an area of 292m peoples ('Euro-land'). Indeed, in early December 1998, interest rates were lowered across the zone to 3%, by way of preparation.

Britain and EMU

EMU raises the issue of a two-speed Europe with variable geometry. In other words, certain countries on certain issues, might move ahead to integration, whereas others might be left behind. As the EU enlarges, it may be that there is an inner core committed to a faster pace of integration. On this issue, Britain is not in the fast lane, although since the advent of the Blair Administration there is a much more positive indication that entry into EMU is 'on the cards' within a few years, once there is a wider acceptance of its desirability and inevitability.

For Labour, the case for entry is an economic matter, to be judged on whether or not 'the time is ripe'. It is felt that to go ahead when economic circumstances are not propitious could be harmful. For many Conservatives, their opposition - not just in this Parliament but for the one after as well - is a matter of sovereignty. EMU involves the transfer of powers hitherto exercised exclusively by governments to an independent European Central Bank, including the right to authorise issues of currency, and determine interest rates. The loss of national flexibility is unacceptable to them. The

Hague leadership believes that its reservations have been justified, given the unimpressive performance of the Euro in its early months of operation.

Under John Major, British policy was to 'wait and see'. It has developed into 'prepare and decide'. The policy has critics on both sides. Euro-sceptics suggest that Tony Blair is covertly taking the country towards membership without admitting his true intent. The pro-single currency camp want to see a stronger lead. However, on an issue on which the public is so wary, he doesn't wish to jeopardise Labour's chances of re-election.

There is a growing feeling among many business people that whether the British like it or not, they will have to join the Euro to remain a force in Europe. Many are predicting a single currency via the back door, as an increasing number of the larger British shops are likely to accept the new notes and coins for fear of losing business from overseas customers.

The Advantages and Disadvantages of a Single Currency for Britain
For private individuals and companies, there are advantages in a single currency and monetary policy. No longer would it be necessary for travellers or business people to change money from one currency into another, which means that transactions can be eased and that losses on currency dealings ended. It is also anticipated that sterling would be less vulnerable to speculation which has dogged it in the past, and that businessmen would benefit from the certainty of what this might involve. Finally, it is believed that interest rates in Britain are likely to be lower over the long term.

Opponents of a single currency wish to cling to the pound sterling, believing that control over the currency is a sign of national sovereignty. They do not wish to see economic policy dictated by a Central Bank, with the British Government having only a marginal impact on its conduct. They realise that key decisions on interest rates would pass out of British hands.

Does EMU matter?

The implications of EMU are far-reaching, for its creation is arguably the biggest step forward for Europe since the Marshall Plan laid the foundations for economic recovery in the aftermath of the Second World War. For the optimists, if all goes to plan monetary union will lay the foundations for the renaissance of Europe, after 25 years of under-performance which has seen the EU's growth rate drop from 3% per annum in the 1970s to 1.8% in the

1990s. They believe that in an era of global economic forces, only the large and powerful can survive. For the pessimists, EMU is a huge risk. They believe that the economies involved are not truly congruent, and that the criteria have been applied in a too liberal manner. They worry that the ECB will have a deflationary bias, that it will keep interest rates too high, will ultimately fail and in so doing imperil the European economy - and in so doing drag other countries outside such as Britain, down with it.

The convergence criteria and the British performance

As applied to the issue of the single currency, the term Convergence refers to the coming together of the economies of the states of the European Union. At Maastricht, convergence criteria were laid down, against which the performances of individual countries could be measured. These were:

i. A high degree of price stability
ii. The elimination of 'excessive' public sector deficits
iii. The observance of the 'normal fluctuation margins' provided for in the Exchange rate Mechanism for at least two years, with no devaluation against the currency of any other member state
iv. The level of long-term interest rates which must not exceed by more than 2% the average of interest rates in the three best-performing states.

NB Given the dilution of the original ERM after the currency problems of the Autumn 1992, the third one was seen as the least important.

Determinants of the British approach to EMU under Labour

For Gordon Brown as Chancellor, there were potential benefits for Britain of a successful single currency, in terms of trade, transparency of costs and currency stability. He told the House of Commons (October 27, 1997) that in principle he favoured British participation. However, his assessment of the case for entry would depend upon five factors:

i. Whether there was a sustainable convergence between Britain and the other economies
ii. Whether there was sufficient flexibility to cope with economic change
iii. The effect on investment
iv. The impact on the financial services industry
v. The impact on employment.

By these tests, Britain could not meet the tests in time for 1999, and therefore entry was not in our economic interest. There was no proper convergence between the British and other European economies, so that entry would have meant accepting a monetary policy which was good for the others but not for Britain. This was the most important determinant. While Britain was in late 1997 in its sixth year of recovery, the rest of Europe was only beginning to emerge from a long recession. As a result, base rates were more than twice as high in Britain than in France or Germany.

EMU did not have an easy birth, and there were times - particularly in the early 1990s, with the Exchange Rate Mechanism in a state of near collapse - when it looked as though it might be still-born. But gestation is now over, and 1999 witnessed an historic breakthrough.

The Social Chapter

There was little in the Treaty of Rome concerning social policy, and member states were left to make their own arrangements. Not until the mid 1980s was the topic of an agreed Community policy of social protection placed high on the agenda. It was the passing of the Single European Act which led to new thinking in this area.

Jacques Delors, as President of the Commission, took the view that the EC must be more than a common market. He wanted to see it evolve as 'an organised space governed by commonly agreed rules that (will) ensure economic and social cohesion, and equality of opportunity'. To this end, the Commission asked the Economic and Social Committee to produce a document setting out social rights which merited protection. The original Charter of Fundamental Social rights, much modified at the insistence of the British Government, later became the Social Chapter.

The Social Chapter was written in as a protocol of the Maastricht Treaty. Britain representatives did not approve of it, somewhat to the surprise of some continental spokespersons who saw its provisions as innocuous, more a codification of existing practice than a definite programme to be achieved within a specified period of time. At best, to them it seemed to represent little more than a series of aspirations to be worked towards over the coming years.

Article 1 of the Agreement committed the eleven other countries who were then members of the European Community to 'the promotion of employment, improved living and working conditions, proper social protection, dialogue between management and labour, the development of human resources with a view to lasting high employment and the combating of exclusion'. At the same time, it was agreed that account should be taken of 'the diverse forms of national practices...and the need to maintain the competitiveness of the Community economy'.

The countries which joined the European Union in 1995 all accepted the Social Protocol, and the new Labour Government in Britain soon announced that it would sign the Agreement. This was done in June 1997, so that all 15 members now accept the original document and any policies agreed under its terms. As a result of the Amsterdam Treaty, the substance of the Protocol is now part of the Treaty of Rome.

The Social Chapter is more of an enabling mechanism than a long list of demands that must be met by business immediately. Only two directives have been passed under its terms so far. The first piece of legislation enacted was the requirement that large multi-national firms establish a mechanism for consultation with their employees, the so-called European Works Councils (EWCs). The second concerned arrangements for parental leave, so ensuring that all working parents are entitled to three month's unpaid absence after the birth of their child.

Britain and the Social Chapter
From the time the idea that Jacques Delors first mooted the idea, the Conservative Government of Margaret Thatcher (and later John Major) disliked the notion of any 'social dimension' to the single market. She denounced it as a 'socialist charter...full of unnecessary controls and regulations', and ever since then Conservatives have criticised the Social Chapter as it emerged at Maastricht as burdensome to industry, imposing costs which would make manufacturing uncompetitive and therefore ultimately increase unemployment in Britain. For them, it represented 'socialism by the back door' or, in the more lurid terms of some opponents, 'creeping Marxism'.

At Maastricht, an opt-out was negotiated by John Major, with the result that the proposals were taken out of the draft Treaty and signed as a separate Social Protocol by the other eleven states. The opt-out was seen as a triumph by the then Prime Minister, and his 'success' in achieving it was politically useful to him, enabling him to portray himself as 'strong' in defence of British interests and to divert attention from other aspects of the Maastricht Treaty which his party supporters might find unpalatable.

Labour and most Liberal Democrat MPs viewed the Social Chapter differently, and approved of the rights which its supporters were urging, such as extended maternity rights, better provision for child-care and fairer treatment for part-time workers. As the main opposition party, Labour wanted to see British workers enjoy the same rights experienced by workers elsewhere. It denounced as 'Euro-Luddites' those right-wing politicians who feared social progress and cared little about the social rights of working people.

Labour took the view that in a single market it was necessary that there should be harmonised social legislation to ensure that workers were adequately covered. The case for such measures had been put before the TUC in 1989 by Jacques Delors, and it was his visit which weaned the party from its anti-Europeanism. The party was keen to embrace just the sort of legislation that Margaret Thatcher had been abandoning throughout the 1980s.

Once in office, Tony Blair was able to demonstrate his pro-European credentials by signing Britain up at an early opportunity. At Amsterdam, he secured agreement that its provisions should be implemented over two years.

Conservatives continue to criticise the Government's policy. Whilst they admit that the Chapter has had only a limited impact so far, they fear that it opens the door for other European social directives that could cost jobs.

The Common Foreign and Security Policy

The early proposals for a European Defence Community and a European Political Community put forward under the **Pleven Plan** proved abortive, and were eventually abandoned in 1954. They were very ambitious and would have taken the Western European participants a long way down the road towards what Monnet called 'the federation of Europe'. Thereafter cooperation was much looser, and although there was a Western European Union to develop the habit of working together on an intergovernmental basis, there was no element of supranational thinking of the kind which Pleven planned.

Members of the European Economic Community recognised that governments could usefully consult with each other. At The Hague (1969), it was agreed that foreign ministers of The Six should draw up proposals for political unification, and the Davignon Report which came out in 1970 made recommendations which according to its authors marked 'the first practical endeavours to demonstrate to all that Europe has a political vocation'. They were adopted, and, intergovernmental in character, the meetings arranged thereafter were the beginning of **European Political Cooperation (EPC)**.

From the 1970s onwards, an attempt was made to harmonise foreign policies, via EPC. There were some successes, but even when agreement was reached there were often underlying tensions which meant that action was based on the lowest common denominator. Circumstances were often difficult, so that at the time of the Falklands War discussion over the admission of Spain (which had close links with Latin America) made a co-ordinated response less effective. The real problem was and remains that issues of foreign and security policy go to the heart of the sovereignty debate. No country will lightly cede any significant degree of independence in these areas.

In 1986, the process of EPC was finally granted Treaty status, when it was incorporated into the Single European Act. However, little was done at that stage to 'put flesh on the bones', and the promise made was no more than a willingness 'to co-ordinate their positions more closely on the political and economic aspects of security'. It was left to the Maastricht summiteers to move cooperation forward, and the 1991 Treaty marks the formal end of EPC and the beginning in its place of the Common Foreign and Security Policy (CFSP).

Maastricht and beyond

The Treaty agreed in December 1991 created the Common Foreign and Security Policy as a second pillar, and in addition gave an enhanced role to the Western European Union as a key defence component along with NATO. A distinction was made between cooperation/coordination and joint action. The European Council decides the areas for joint action, and is empowered 'to define the principles and general guidelines for the common foreign and security policy'. This guidance is translated into detailed but still unanimous decisions by the foreign ministers of each member state. They can designate certain procedural areas of implementation for subsequent majority voting.

These arrangements apply to foreign and security policy, but more detail is provided in the Maastricht Treaty on security matters. It is envisaged that the CFSP will in time involve 'the framing of a common defence policy, which might in time lead to a common defence'. The WEU is seen as 'an integral part of the development of the Union' and has an important role which is defined as being 'to elaborate and implement decisions and actions of the Union which have defence implications'. This effectively makes it an executive arm of the EU, although it is technically an independent and distinct body.

The settlement at Maastricht allows member countries to deal with essentially bilateral matters with little reference to other states (e.g., Britain and Hong Kong). However, if there is the political will for common action the procedures available allow such cooperation to operate.

At **Amsterdam**, the CFSP was taken a stage forward. The European Council can now move beyond laying down 'principles...and general guidelines', but also adopt 'common strategies'. The secretariat of the CFSP is strengthened, and the Secretary-General of the Council of Ministers becomes the 'High Representative' for the policy. There was discussion at Amsterdam of making the Secretary-General the 'Mr/Mrs CFSP', as part of a bid to provide the policy with a 'human face' and give the EU a more clear and meaningful voice in world affairs. This would have significantly strengthened the position and made it comparable to that of Secretary-General of NATO or of the United Nations. The proposal failed to make the final text.

There is no-one who can speak, let alone act, on Europe's behalf, a point made by an American Secretary of State back in the 1970s when he asked 'When I want to speak to Europe, whom do I call?'. Europe speaks with different voices, and there tends to be a lack of clear thinking and of any unified approach in tackling matters of overseas policy. Hence the squabbling which can occur, what Jacques Delors referred to as 'organised schizophrenia'.

Some member states would like to go further than the present arrangements. They want to see foreign and security policies made more efficient, and believe that a well-funded policy-formulating unit, led by a high profile figure, would be a useful start in representing the EU's policies to the rests of the world. Some wish to see the development of common policies including the eventual framing of a common defence policy, with ultimately the creation of a European Army. However, many supporters of the CFSP recognise the difficulty of achieving any real progress until there is a greater degree of political union in Europe.

Britain and the CFSP

Britain's global role in the early post-war years inevitably made its statesmen unwilling to commit themselves fully to any move towards a harmonisation of policy in defence and foreign affairs. Given its record of independence, they were reluctant to surrender any sovereignty in this area. For instance, the Conservatives were not prepared to join the European Defence Community, and should the plan have been implemented would have remained aloof. They preferred their own proposal, the creation of the intergovernmental WEU, which actually went ahead.

Over issues such as the Falklands War, there was some initial consultation with our European partners and modest agreement on an economic response. But there was no common foreign policy, and although there was supportive action from European (and rather more from America) policy-makers, Britain acted alone. Again, over the Gulf War in 1991, Britain and America were the key players, and Euro-sceptics took the view that Community inaction proved that there was no real European defence or foreign policy.

At Maastricht, the whole issue of relationships with the United States and the wider international community was debated, as well as the substance of European political union. The British feared that the French President, Mitterrand, was keen to distance Europe from American power and influence, rather as de Gaulle had once done. The French believed that Britain's attitude to issues of defence reflected its ambiguity to the whole European enterprise, claiming that the British with their Atlanticist leanings could not make up their mind about their national priorities. He believed that a common foreign policy was meaningless without a common defence policy, a view from which Britain dissented.

British representatives made the distinction between security policy which it was right for the EC to define on an intergovernmental basis, and defence policy proper. Security involves a wider network of agreements to make war less likely, whereas defence is primarily a matter of how nations defend themselves when under attack. Britain rejected the idea that there could be any move to greater European control of defence matters.

Since Maastricht, British policy-makers have continued to resist further developments in foreign and security policy. There is as yet little difference between Labour and Conservative policies in this area. Although the present Government is keen to prove that it is an active player on the European stage this does not mean that it is willing to surrender Britain's freedom of manoeuvre over these sensitive aspects of national policy.

There are many difficulties in the path of policy-makers in the overseas and defence fields. Countries each have their national interests to pursue, and agreement among 15 countries is difficult to achieve. History, tradition and

---

Developments in cooperation: straws in the wind?

There are, however, some signs of change. Robin Cook is reported[3] as favouring the creation of an EU Rapid Reaction Unit to be on permanent stand-by for emergencies. He wants member states to offer the Commission a list of the kind of humanitarian and other resources which could be provided at overnight notice His concern was that there should be a quicker Brussels response to crisis situations such as that which occurred as the first wave of refugees fled from Kosova.

The new External Affairs Commissioner, Chris Patten, has already argued for closer military co-operation. Speaking to the European Parliament for the first time, his personal manifesto included the plea that European tax-payers should be persuaded to pay more for their armed forces and that a Euro-corps could be operational 'in the not-too-distant-future'. For him, the Kosovan crisis pointed to Europe's need for an enhanced defence capability under the NATO umbrella. This meant 'credible defence forces that [could] be brought together quickly', rather than the immediate creation of a common European army.

Robin Cook is alleged[4] to have gone further. In proposals which build largely on un-noticed defence co-operation between London and Paris in recent years, he and fellow foreign ministers are said to have endorsed plans to abolish the Western European Union and create 'effective EU decision-making in the field of security and defence policy' and an 'EU military committee'. Internal documents have stressed the need for credible military capability' and envisage regular meetings of defence ministers and military staff. The Foreign Secretary also favours regular meetings of senior officials from EU national governments to co-ordinate practical measures and monitor the development of a common foreign and security policy.

131
●●●

present realities combine to make them wish to assert their own national identities, rather than act in concert with their European neighbours. It is therefore not surprising that coordination and action have been difficult to achieve in foreign and security matters.

Britain is not unique in wishing to retain control in its own hands, but its historical and emotional ties make it especially difficult for leaders to commit the country to a solely European involvement. As the EU unfolds, the CFSP - and in particular harmonisation of defence policy - is an area where the British ambiguity about Europe is likely to be further put to the test (but see the box on the previous page).

CONCLUSION

Some of the main EU policy areas were the subject of decisions made a long time ago, some have been the result of more recent initiatives and some are still evolving. Here we have spotlighted four which are particularly important and which have loomed large in the debates surrounding Britain's place in the Union.

Even where there is a substantial degree of Brussels involvement, it does not follow that a coherent common policy results from a common approach, for it can be difficult to reconcile conflicting national interests and preferences. Member states have their own traditions and problems, and the fight to preserve national interests in particular policy areas can make it difficult to achieve a genuinely co-ordinated and consistent EU approach.

The balance sheet of Britain's membership

INTRODUCTION

Britain's membership of, and role in, the European Community, was much contested in the early 1960s, 1970s, 1980s and 1990s. The issues have differed, but many of the same people who worked for entry originally continue to emphasise a European approach to the conduct of our affairs, and those who took a contrary view have seen their worst fears confirmed. However, along the road, there have been significant changes in the attitudes of some politicians and parties.

The Conservatives were originally more enthusiastic for membership and remained so until the late 1970s, whilst the Labour leadership was lukewarm, its supporters often hostile to the whole concept. In the Thatcher years, ministers displayed a coolness towards our European partners. Labour saw an opportunity to outflank them on European policy, and at the end of the decade it seized the political advantage by reversing the anti-EC stand it had once taken.

In between the fervently pro and strongly anti positions, there are many who feel that membership was, and still is, appropriate, there being no realistic alternative. However, they may be disappointed at the way things have turned out, and perhaps feel that the movement towards closer cooperation has gone too far, too fast.

Britain has now had nearly three decades of membership, and the process of adaptation has influenced many aspects of our national life. It has not been an easy ride for governments or peoples.

ASK YOURSELF

- Why did leading politicians of all parties come to see advantages in membership of the European Community once they were in office?
- What did supporters of membership hope that Britain would gain from joining?
- In what respects has membership proved a disappointment for those who once argued strongly in favour of Britain taking its place in the Community?
- What benefits has membership given Britain?
- Is there a future for Britain outside the European Union?

MAIN TEXT

The case FOR membership

For ardent pro-Europeans, the case has always been a **Political** one. British leaders recognised that, after centuries of fratricidal strife on the continent, others were making an attempt to resolve old conflicts, and lay the ghosts of the past. Such a reconciliation, particularly between the old rivals, France and Germany, was essential if Europe was to be strong and free. European statesmen saw a link between post-war economic reconstruction and political reconciliation. It was recognised that no one country could prosper on its own, and that an effort to achieve unity in Europe was a priority. In this way, Europe would carry weight in international relations and be a stabilising influence in the world. United, Europe could play a role in the improvement of international relations, and not be dwarfed by the Super-powers, the USSR and the USA, and the emerging countries such as Japan and eventually China.

The development of The Six and now The Fifteen has made Europe a respected force in the world, so that other Powers and developing countries are prepared to deal with the Union rather than individual states. Its size and population give it great significance. If ever US commitment to the continent should weaken, it can survive on its own.

The question for Britain was whether it could afford to be sidelined from these developments. In former years, it might have dreamed of playing a world role, mediating in disputes of the day, but by the 1960s, its influence was waning; Britain was no longer in the front rank of European powers. As a shrewd American observer, Dean Acheson, put it in 1962: 'Britain has lost an empire, but not yet found a role'. Europe offered such a role, as the other elements of the 'three circles' counted for less.

Edward Heath was aware of the linkage of economic and political goals for the Community, and saw that by economic means the political objectives might be achieved. He believed that:

Our purpose in creating the new Europe is political. Let us never lose sight of that fact. It is to prevent Europe from being destroyed either from within or without; to create the prosperity which will ensure support for democratic institutions; to provide the economic growth on which to base its security.

For him, and for early supporters of entry, the case was essentially political. As Macmillan once put it, the issues were more significant than a petty squabble over the price of butter! In 1967 Wilson shared this view arguing that: 'Europe is now faced with the opportunity of a great move forward in political unity, and we can - and indeed must - play our full part in it'.

Exactly how close that unity would become, and where it would lead, was unknown, but the dream of ever-closer-union has always been the vision of Euro-enthusiasts on the continent, and of the most committed supporters in Britain. In the face of such a vision, supporters were unconcerned about any loss of sovereignty in Britain, for as the White Paper put it, in 1971:

There is no question of Britain losing essential national sovereignty. What is proposed is a sharing and an enlargement of individual national sovereignties in the common interest.

In such an organisation, Britain would have an opportunity to make its views heard, and its influence felt. Any loss of independence was more than balanced by the opportunity for greater influence over the course of events in Europe. Harold Lever, a one-time Labour MP and minister put the point well: 'We should beware of clinging to a nominal sovereignty at a cost of losing a real and effective control over our destiny which we might have co-operatively if we pooled it'.

For enthusiasts today, the political arguments in favour of European unity are the overwhelming considerations. In the past two decades, the progress has not been as great as some would have hoped. Europe has not always spoken with one voice, and so they want to see it develop into something which is more than a forum where the Heads of Government meet and discuss problems and ideas. To them, it is a community to which nations have handed over an amount of decision making, so that decisions can be taken jointly, and to the benefit of all. At the very least, this implies close cooperation. For some enthusiasts, it is a reason for going ahead to build a real 'United States of Europe'.

The **Economic** case for joining the EC was that Britain wanted to benefit from the large market that The Six had created. It was felt that British manufacturers would be able to produce more cheaply because of economies of scale, and sell more of their goods in this dynamic and expanding free-trade area. The competition that British industrialists would be subjected to was thought to be bracing, encouraging efficient production. As a result of these new business opportunities, the nation's prosperity would be secured, and improved living standards would result. The White Paper made the point that in the years after the formation of the Community up to 1969, the average income in The Six had risen by 75%, in Britain by 40%.

In the Referendum campaign, such arguments were re-emphasised, and part of the case for staying-in was also the disruption involved in pulling out. The 'Yes' campaigners stressed that membership offered the best framework for success and the best protection for our standard of living, that the USA and the Commonwealth wanted us to remain in, and that outside there was a harsh, cold world in which Britain would find itself dangerously isolated with none of our friends offering to revive old partnerships.

25 years later, even some supporters may feel that some of the claims were over-optimistic. The increased opportunities for British industrialists have not generated the steady economic growth and prosperity anticipated, but most of British industry is today geared to Europe as the main outlet. Several companies now have bases in Europe; GEC plants turn out products in a number of member countries, and others such as Rank Hovis McDougall and Rank Xerox have put a lot of time and effort into building up sales in Europe.

By 1980-1, trade with the EC had produced a positive trade balance, though since then it has been less favourable. Exports to the rest of the world have gone up much less than those to the EC; between 1972-87, the proportion of Britain's exports going to other members of the Community rose from 34-49%, that going to the Commonwealth fell from 19-12%. For many of these years, the overall terms of trade were assisted by a substantial surplus in our oil trade, though in many goods Britain fared better with Europe than with Japan and the United States.

The benefits of staying in

At a time when the Maastricht Treaty was being debated by the House of Commons, John Major told MPs that membership had been good for Britain and Europe:

It was right to join, not just for the opportunities that the Community offers as a common market, not even for the economic strength of the Community collectively, but for the collective power of the European democracies to improve the general weight, politically and economically, of European opinion throughout the world. Nothing that has happened in the almost 20 years of our membership causes me to doubt the rightness of the original decision to join the Community.

In 1996, his Conservative Government produced a White Paper outlining its stance on Europe. It described the EU as 'central to our economic prospects' and politically as 'the basis upon which we must consolidate democracy and prosperity across the whole of Europe'. Such a case has been reiterated by many other pro-Europeans as well. Tony Blair has stressed[1] that 'millions of jobs depend on it. Europe is vital to Britain's trade'. Adair Turner of the CBI has ridiculed[2] 'the idea that there is a prosperous future for a Britain detached from membership...if we let this debate spin out of control towards anti-European delusions, the Germans could end up with our investment and jobs'.

Many British jobs do now depend on trade with the Union and would be threatened if we lost access to it. Similarly, the flow of inward investment has to some extent come about because Britain is seen as a gateway to Europe. Its proximity to other EU markets and relatively good labour relations, make it an attractive location, and the 'Invest in Britain Bureau' of the Department of Trade and Industry encourages new projects. For many years, Britain has been the leading country for US manufacturing

137

> **A Conservative case for Europe**
>
> Europe is an opportunity. We need to come to terms with its competitive thrust and to win our place within an enlarged market. Outside the market we could face that same competition and would have to watch it bestow ever greater benefits upon the Community's members which would be denied to us...
>
> On our own, we could expect a diminishing influence in world affairs, both in trade and foreign policy: as part of the Community, we speak as the largest economic unit in the world...
>
> Inside Europe, we are part of what will be a world power. The national sovereignty which we lose is more than made good by a share of the much larger sovereignty which we get from participation in Europe. Our imperial days are over, and while we cannot rule Europe in place of our Empire we should be an influential senior partner...
>
> The movement towards a Europe whose citizens are free to exercise their professional skills and to sell their wares from Antrim to Athens without seeking officialdom's leave will recover for Britain a sense of partnership in a shared destiny.
>
> *Extracts from Where There's a Will (Hutchinson, 1987), by Michael Heseltine, MP and former senior minister.*

investment in Europe, and around 30% of Japanese investment in the EU comes here, in the form of Hitachi factories in South Wales, and Nissan and Toyota ones in England, among many other schemes. Outside the Union, Britain would be less attractive base for such investment.

Overall, as Adair Turner has argued[3], British industry is now economically integrated with the EU, and dependent upon it: 'The single market has brought major benefits to Britain and Europe'. Outside the EU, British exporters 'would have to comply with regulations and standards over which British governments would have had no control, and would find that a Little England stance left the country dangerously isolated and exposed'.

Moreover, apart from access to a vast market for industry, there are opportunities for British citizens to work in the Union - a more realistic possibility since the passage of the Single European Act and the standardisation of qualifications. Rather more British citizens benefit from the funds established by the EU to help various groups of workers who have suffered from the impact of economic change. Such funds cover agriculture, social aid, and regional development.

Examples of EU funding for projects around Britain. At the top, a derelict Derbyshire farm is turned into a centre for cottage industry. In the middle, old waterway buildings in Blackburn become a business venue. At the bottom, a new bridge across the river Loughor improves the Swansea-Llanelli road.

Reproduced with the kind permission of the European Parliament, UK office.

The EU awards grants and loans from various sources. The European Regional Development Fund (ERDF) plays an important part in regional development in Britain. Four areas qualify for Objective One assistance. Cornwall and the Isles of Scilly, Merseyside, West Wales and South Yorkshire will share £3b. between 2000 and 2006; they are deemed to be among the poorest areas, lagging behind the rest of the Union. Objective Two aid is for areas facing industrial or rural decline, whilst Objective Three targets training and projects to develop workers' skills.

Northern Ireland and the Highlands and Islands lost Objective One status from the end of 1999, but gained compensation aid packages of some £825m. and £200m. respectively. In all, the UK will get almost £1.5b. a year, some 8.5% of the total spending of the structural funds.

What Britain gets from the EU: a summary

- Free access to the large market of the EU (315m, excluding UK), as well as that of EFTA, now linked in the EEA.
- Inward investment.
- Opportunities for British workers to live and work in the Union.
- Substantial grants and loans from the Structural Funds.
- Influence in world affairs, acting as part of a large trading bloc.
- Opportunities via the EU to assist developing countries.

See also p146-48 for a summary of what funding Britain gets out of the Union.

The case AGAINST membership

Early critics of entry were particularly anxious about the impact of food prices at home, and on Commonwealth suppliers of many basic commodities - e.g., Caribbean sugar and New Zealand dairy products. Britain would lose its trading ties with markets such as New Zealand, and its freedom to buy where it could at the cheapest rates. They were unconvinced about the beneficial effects of exposure to the chill winds of competition, and claimed that Britain's relatively slow growth in the 1950s and 1960s had little to do with membership of the Community; there were strong economies both inside and outside The Six.

In 1975, the 'No' campaigners claimed that all of the promises made at the time of accession had proved illusory - the rise in our living standards, more investment, better productivity, faster industrial growth, more employment, a trade surplus with the EC members, had not come about. Since Britain joined, prices had risen because Britain could no longer buy goods in the cheapest markets in the world. The alternative they posed was for Britain to remain part of EFTA, and through that organisation to trade with the other EC members without incurring the costs of membership.

By the early 1980s, a decade after entry, many felt that their fears had been confirmed. They were alarmed at Britain's unfair Budgetary contributions, which meant that Britain was putting in much more to the Community than it got out. Agricultural spending via the CAP was foremost in their criticism, for it was felt that Britain was subsidising inefficient farming in France and to a lesser extent Germany. The result of the guaranteed prices that these farmers were given was the creation of the notorious beet and butter mountains which were often ridiculed and condemned.

A Labour case against Europe

In 1975, Tony Benn wrote an open letter to his constituents at the time of the Referendum debate. In it, he spelt out his constitutional objections to membership of the Community:

First, it subjects us to laws and taxes which your members of Parliament do not enact, such laws and taxes being enacted by authorities you do not directly elect and cannot dismiss through the ballot box.

Secondly, British membership means that Community laws and taxes cannot be changed or repealed by the British people...

Thirdly, the EEC requires the British courts to uphold and enforce Community laws that have not been passed by Parliament, and... Parliament cannot change or amend [them]...

Fourthly, British membership imposes duties and constraints upon British governments not deriving from the British Parliament...

Fifthly, British membership, by permanently transferring sovereign legislative and financial powers to the Community authorities... permanently insulates [those] authorities from direct control by the British electors who cannot dismiss them and whose views, therefore, need carry no weight with them...

Of course, because Britain did not join the Community at its inception, the organisation was not devised - and nor did it develop - with specifically British interests in mind. Late-comers to the club could not expect that members would suddenly change everything for their benefit. Certainly, the industrial and trade advantages which optimists had spoken of did not quickly materialise, for Britain had the misfortune to join just as the 1973 oil crisis dropped Western Europe into a cycle of stagnation which lasted for several years.

Today, many erstwhile critics have accepted membership as inevitable though they continue to believe that Britain would have fared better outside rather than inside the Community.

Opponents of entry do not deny that the Union has been good for the six countries which were the pioneers of the original Community, and that it has been instrumental in ending the dispute between France and Germany. They doubt the wisdom of Britain being part of the arrangement. They worry about the loss of Parliamentary Sovereignty, and lament the inability of Britain to control its own destiny. They believe that Britain loses much of its freedom of manoeuvre, for decisions are increasingly taken in Brussels.

Some of the early sceptics envisaged that the European Parliament would be strengthened and directly elected, and that the Commission would use its power to issue regulations binding upon the British people. Direct elections have come about, there has been a (slow) growth in the powers of the Parliament, and the Commission has issued a number of regulations which British governments and some of the British people dislike. It has not been difficult for the popular press to whip up anti-Community/Union feeling, by dwelling on some of its wilder (and often unimplemented) recommendations, such as those seeking to change the name of chocolate to 'vegelate' or to change the title of much British ice-cream.

Opponents doubt if membership has been good for Britain, a point expressed by former Chancellor, Norman Lamont, who claims[4] to be 'unable to discern any benefits from Britain's EU membership'. He and others of similar views stress the costs of membership, in particular the budgetary contributions over some twenty five years. He also notes that 'from the moment when Britain decided to tie itself to Europe, the European economy became one of the slowest-growing in the world'.

Sceptics also pour scorn on two other arguments advanced by pro-Europeans. They say that the old argument used in favour of membership,

British access to a tariff-free trading zone, no longer applies. Successive rounds of the GATT (now World Trade Organisation) talks have all but eliminated tariffs as a significant barrier to trade, and outside the Union there would be little worry about the difficulty of doing business with our European neighbours. In addition, they are unconvinced by the argument about inward investment. They stress that Japanese investment has come to Britain primarily because of lower costs of employment, a low level of corporate taxation, political and social stability, and comparatively honest public administration. Europe has not been a key factor, and indeed Britain's agreement to the Social Chapter and likely future involvement in a single currency could actually make investment less attractive.

As to the alternatives to membership, the Norwegian option is perhaps the most feasible. Involvement in the European Economic Area (EEA) would give full access to Europe's single market, but without any of the integrationist disadvantages. Norway has experienced strong growth, and those who advocate this position say that the Norwegians appear to be getting the best of both worlds - the benefits but not the pitfalls of the European Union.

It was Enoch Powell, an advocate of the 'Parliamentary Sovereignty' argument, who suggested that: 'The alternative to the Common Market is like the alternative to suicide - don't do it'. He and others believed that Britain could survive on its own. As the 'No' booklet in the Referendum put it: 'Let's rule ourselves, while trading and remaining friendly with other nations'. Many Euro-sceptics would still endorse such a view.

What membership costs Britain

- A contribution to the running costs, with the prospect of always being a net contributor to the Union, and possibly losing the rebate.
- Free access for EU businessmen to British markets.

- Free access to the peoples of the Union to the British labour market.
- Disadvantageous policies such as the CAP, seen as enormously expensive as well as wasteful.
- Regular balance of payments deficit with the EU.

- Domination by an excessively centralised, undemocratic Brussels and the loss of freedom of manoeuvre.
- A threat to our national identity, with sovereignty being eroded on issues ranging from immigration to fishing, from EMU to the Social Chapter.

Staying in and making it work?

Of course, the Euro-enthusiasts have the advantage that Britain is in the Union, and even if it were desirable, withdrawal would be hard to achieve. It would involve negotiating transitional arrangements and would be a messy business. Britain would surrender any influence over the development of the EU, whilst still finding itself subject to some of the decrees. Most people have accepted that Britain is in it for good, and many of the Euro-sceptics and Euro-phobes are involved in a damage-limitation exercise designed to ensure that Britain retains some freedom of manoeuvre in developing its economy, regulating its currency, and planning its social legislation, defence and foreign affairs.

Ultimately, Britain could withdraw, and this is the element of Parliamentary Sovereignty which remains unaffected. If one Parliament cannot bind its successors, then in the future a government could always bring in legislation to take Britain out of the Union.

CONCLUSION

Britain's membership of the European Union has yielded some benefits, but there have also been real costs. The full effects of British involvement have only been apparent in more recent years, partly because it was some time before the full constitutional implications were appreciated by many observers, and also because there was little forward movement within the Community in the first few years after entry. Over the last decade or so, however, Europe has had an increasingly important impact on British life.

The economic effects have not been as beneficial as was once anticipated, and there is room for argument over the degree of benefit which Britain has experienced. The political bonus is that by acting in concert with other European states, Britain has more influence in the world than would otherwise be the case. This voice is strengthened by the fact that the EU is such a powerful trading bloc in world markets that it carries a considerable clout when any trade negotiations take place.

Such considerations cut little ice as far as the unrepentant doubters are concerned. For them, the promises about the advantages which membership would bring have yet to be fulfilled, and we have experienced all pain and little gain. They do not wish to see more power handed to Brussels or Frankfurt, and instead think that we should be repatriating lost powers back to the British people.

Winners and losers in the European Union

Payments into the EU		**Receipts from EU**	
Actual contributions made (£m)		*What is paid to each country*	
Germany	16,900.1	France	9,725.4
France	10,100.0	Spain	8,554.0
Italy	7,271.4	Germany	8,033.8
UK	6,735.9	Italy	6,130.3
Spain	3,693.7	UK	4,843.0
Netherlands	3,609.8	Greece	4,104.0
Belgium	2,232.2	Portugal	2,995.1
Sweden	1,593.0	Ireland	2,417.4
Austria	1,524.0	Belgium	1,625.0
Denmark	1,106.7	Netherlands	1,618.5
Greece	901.0	Austria	1,302.4
Finland	782.3	Denmark	1,264.1
Portugal	737.4	Sweden	980.5
Ireland	578.0	Finland	788.1
Luxembourg	132.8	Luxembourg	68.3

Basis of calculation for each Member State
- Customs duties on products imported from outside the EU
- Agricultural levies charged at the external frontiers of the EU to bring the price of imported foodstuffs from the rest of the world up to the levels of the Union
- A proportion of the VAT collected in the member states, calculated according to a uniform assessment procedure
- A fourth resource based on the GNP of member states.

Net receipts, as % of GDP

Countries in credit		**Countries in debit**	
Ireland	5.1	Italy	0.01
Luxembourg	4.9	Finland	0.1
Greece	4.1	France	0.1
Portugal	3.1	Netherlands	0.3
Spain	1.2	UK*	0.3
Belgium	0.8	Austria	0.4
Denmark	0.1	Germany	0.6
		Sweden	0.6

* *Not allowing for Fontainebleau rebate.*

Comparative Contributions

Germany accounts for 26.0% of total GDP in the EU, but pays 28.2% of the budget.

France has 17.2% of the GDP, and pays 17.5%.

UK has 16.1% of the GDP, but - because of the rebate - pays only 11.9%.

NB All figure adapted from those appearing in The Guardian, 22.10.1998.

Britain and Europe: the past and the future

INTRODUCTION

Britain joined the EEC fifteen years after it began its operations, twenty years after The Six had pioneered the path to unity. Whereas other late entrants seem to have made the adjustments in attitude required to make a success of membership, this has not been the case for many British people and in particular for some of their elected representatives. The British have found it hard to adapt, hence their reputation on the continent as 'reluctant Europeans'. Perhaps this reflects a national difficulty in coming to terms with Britain's reduced circumstances in the world.

ASK YOURSELF

- Would Britain have been less of an awkward partner in Europe if we had joined The Six at the start of their joint endeavours?
- Is it fair to portray Britain as a 'reluctant European'?
- Is the Labour leadership really any more pro-European than that of previous British governments?
- Should Britain fear a federal Europe?
- Is there a future for Britain outside the European Union?

MAIN TEXT

A global power

In 1945, Britain seemed to be a major Power, though its strength can be overstressed. As a result of this status, change seemed unnecessary. For a long while the British allowed their awareness of the historical and cultural differences between Britain and Europe to predominate over their political judgement. Hugo Young has written[1] perceptively about popular attitudes at the time:

The island people were not only different but, mercifully separate, housed behind their moat...They were also inestimably superior, as was shown by history both ancient and modern: by the resonance of the Empire on which the sun never set, but equally by the immediate circumstances out of which the new Europe was born, the war itself. Her sense of national independence, enhanced by her unique empire, absorbed by all creeds and classes and spoke for by virtually every analyst, could not be fractured...

Since 1945, it has become apparent that Britain's declining economic fortunes have meant that it has not been able to sustain the position it once held. It has been hard to come to terms with that situation. Managing national decline is not a glorious role for politicians, and it is one which arouses little popular enthusiasm. Some people still hanker after the world leadership which was possible in their parents' generation. Many more concede that Britain's capacity to influence events has been much weakened, but are unconvinced that the logic of events should drive the country more closely into the embrace of our continental partners.

For years, Britain still attempted to preserve its global role. Sir Anthony Eden spoke for many of his countrymen when he gave his reasons for not signing up for membership of the EDC. Speaking with the authority of a Foreign Secretary, he observed[2]:

Britain's story and her interests lie far beyond the Continent of Europe. Our thoughts move across the seas to the many communities in which our people play their part, in every corner of the world. These are our family ties. That is our life; without it we should be no more than some millions of people living on an island off the coast of Europe, in which nobody wants to take any particular notice.

Not surprisingly, the country which 'won the war' felt that with such a world-wide importance it could win the peace. It did not need to tie itself in to any commitments with the countries which it had defeated or which had been overrun in the hostilities of World War Two. Britain felt that it could afford to remain aloof from Europe. It was not ready to recognise or admit its increasing weakness.

148
• • •

Such an attitude had deep roots in the British psyche, and it may be considered understandable in the circumstances of the time. However, it was combined with an inability to appreciate the enthusiasm and dedication of other nations to closer integration in pursuit of 'the European idea'. Consistently, British politicians then and in more recent years have underestimated the strength of this determination, and have assumed that carefully constructed measures of intergovernmental cooperation would be a substitute for their more visionary approach.

A change of direction

In 1963, Dean Acheson, a former American Secretary of State, observed that: 'Britain has lost an empire, but not yet found a role'. The comment wounded British pride, but some politicians recognised that it contained more than a little truth. Among them, there was a growing belief that Europe might provide the theatre in which Britain would have the best chance of influencing events and opinions in the world at large.

In the event, as we have seen (see p29-30), Prime Minister Macmillan found it expedient to apply for Britain to join the EEC in 1961, as it became clear that Britain's capacity to influence the outcome of events had been much curtailed. Neither the Commonwealth nor the American connection seemed to count for as much as had been assumed a decade or so before. But not until the retirement of General de Gaulle was British membership welcome to the whole Community.

Apart from a committed band of ardent Europeans, it would be hard to detect widespread enthusiasm for the prospect of entry in 1973. However, there was a fairly general feeling that changes on the world scene and the need for access to the large continental market made accession desirable, even necessary. When the chance came for the British people to express their view (in the referendum of 1975) they showed a strong backing for membership, for once the country had committed itself it was recognised that it might be a cold world outside should it prematurely depart.

Yet there never was popular excitement in Britain about belonging the Community. It was appreciated that it was probably wise and necessary for

Britain to work with our new partners, for the alternatives did not look very promising. The point was well made[3] by FS Northedge:

[The] important thing about British entry into Europe was that it had almost every appearance of being a policy of last resort, adopted, one might almost say, when all other expedients had failed. There was no suggestion of it being hailed as a brilliant success...the impression remained that it was brought about in humiliating circumstances, and when other options in foreign policy had lost their convincingness.

Hugo Young has written[4] similarly of British motives:

For the makers of the original 'Europe', beginning to fulfil Victor Hugo's dream, their creation was a triumph. Out of defeat, they produced a new kind of victory. For Britain, by contrast, the entry into Europe was a defeat: a fate she had resisted, a necessity reluctantly accepted, the last resort of a once great power, never for one moment a climactic or triumphant engagement with the construction of Europe. This has been integral to the national psyche, perhaps only half articulated, since 1973. The sense of the Community as a place of British failure - proof of Britain's failed independence, site of her failed domination - is deep in the undertow of the tides and whirlpools [of Britain's relations with the other European countries].

The point is a fair one. Eurobarometer, the EC's polling organisation, has consistently found that the majority of British respondents favoured closer cooperation in Europe in some form, and recognised the inevitability of further steps along the route to unity, on the right terms. But they are unsure about any move to further integration, a point noted[5] by Geoffrey Martin, the head of the European Commission office in London: 'The British have not seen Europe as an opportunity. They regard it as somewhere between an obligation and a mistake'.

The broad sympathy for British involvement changed after the Maastricht agreement had been signed. The public mood seemed to move in a more Euro-sceptical direction. This may have been a reflection of the outcome of the Danish referendum and of other signs of growing doubt on the continent. It also reflected the lack of a strong pro-European lead from British ministers. Indeed, throughout the period of British membership, public opinion has been very sensitive to the attitudes adopted by political leaders and the media, and also to the turn of events.

Growing doubts

British politicians - even ones who are seen as among the more pro-European - have often expressed a coolness towards their counterparts on the continent. It was Harold Macmillan who wrote[6] to Whitehall officials (shortly before the first British application to join the EEC) that the problem with the European Commission was that it was run by 'the Jews, the planners and the old cosmopolitan element'. He went on to state his fear that the Community would be 'dominated in fact by Germany and used as an instrument for the revival of German power through economic means', which amounted to 'really giving them on a plate what we fought two wars to prevent'.

The author of *Using Europe, Abusing the Europeans*, Wolfram Kaiser, shows[7] that the 'British tradition of using Europe [as an instrument of policy] and abusing the Europeans [for failing to get its way]' has a long history. The tactic intensified during the era of Conservative rule after 1979. In the Tory years, there was a developing scepticism in the Governmental approach to relations with Europe, at times a distinct frostiness. John Major, usually regarded as more sympathetic to Europe than his predecessor, nonetheless resorted to obstruction accompanied by accusations of bad faith, whereas the Euro-sceptic Lord Tebbit was moved to describe[8] the EU as 'a bunch of liars and cheats'.

Whilst Conservative leaders were concerned to stress and expand the role of the Community as a free trade area, their continental partners often had a different long term agenda. Their vision was of a Community in which the degree of union became ever-closer, and this was written into the small print of the treaties. For several years, the full implications of membership were not fully realised in Britain. Even those who were involved in the negotiations and signed up for the next stage in the road to unity sometimes had an inadequate grasp of the detail contained therein. This was particularly the case with Margaret Thatcher who by supporting the Single European Act committed Britain to what has been described[9] as 'a milestone on the federalist road'.

British ministers - especially during Mrs Thatcher's Premiership - sought to fashion the Community along the lines set out in her Bruges speech of September 1988. Rejecting any form of European super-state, she reminded her listeners of Britain's contribution to the liberation of Europe in 1944-45 and offered a description of how the Community might develop in the future. Her remarks cast her firmly in the Gaullist mould, for she made it clear that it was neither possible nor desirable to 'suppress nationhood and concentrate power at the centre of a European conglomerate'. She favoured 'willing and active cooperation between independent states', and wanted to see Europe speak with a more united voice. But this must be done in such a way that it 'preserves the different traditions, Parliamentary powers and sense of national pride in one's own country. It was apparent that she had little or no sympathy with talk of a European Idea. She was no utopian, but took the view that Europe could be made to work to Britain's advantage - as long as British leaders made a firm stand against Community interference and regulation, and were determined to concentrate attention on developing a deregulated market in Europe.

Her successor, John Major, for all of his initial wish to see Britain 'at the heart of Europe' was forced to recognise that within his party there was little sympathy for extending British commitments within the Union. He sought to limit its competence, and delay making any decisions which bound Britain more closely to the other member states. For after the Maastricht ratification, enthusiasm among the Conservatives distinctly cooled on matters European, and several polls indicated that public opinion was similarly lukewarm on closer ties. Indeed, the issue of the single currency and the adequacy of the British opt-out was a matter of continuing debate. Rather than sign up for a closer commitment, there are some people now willing to contemplate a future for Britain outside the Union.

An about turn?

In Opposition, Tony Blair said he would never let Britain be isolated in Europe, a remark which was much derided by some Conservative ministers who claimed that he would sell out essential national interests. When he entered Downing Street, there were many optimists who hoped that the sometimes icy relationship with Europe would thaw. There could be a fresh start, with an internationalist, pro-European government in office. The process of building support for the European Union might begin.

The jury is still out. In Europe, where there was some sympathy for Britain's position over the Euro, doubts have nonetheless been expressed as to whether the Prime Minister is really willing to start developing a more pro-European constituency. The rhetoric from London is generally more communautaire, but there have been suggestions from some continental leaders suggesting that Tony Blair has been unwilling to really try and sell the European cause - and particularly the single currency - to the electorate. Also, when issues such as the handling of Saddam Hussein (Iraq) or Slobodan Milosevic (Serbia) have emerged, the Blair reflex has been to turn to the Americans rather than seek to consult with and rally European opinion. There may have been good reasons for acting as he did, but in continental eyes it sometimes seems as though he should prove his European credentials in action as well as in words. Doubters note that he regularly reveals a preference for Washington over Brussels, and that his relationship with Bill Clinton seems to be more important than his ties with European leaders.

Furthermore from a European perspective, it does seem on occasion as though the old British habit of lecturing the Europeans has continued. At an early stage in his Premiership, Tony Blair urged his pragmatic and free-market variety of social democracy as the best way forward for the EU. Some saw as arrogance the fact that they were being lectured by a new arrival in the Union club, even if the speaker was one of the more charismatic and genial politicians on the European stage.

Europe has been a difficult area of policy for British politicians for many years. More recently, it has been something of a political football in the party battle, and those who exhibit signs of pro-European attitudes and policies tend to face a barrage of adverse media criticism in the tabloid press at home. As we have already quoted (see p59-60), David Butler and Simon Westlake make the point[10] that Euroscepticism has a long history; 'If there is a European "problem", it is not restricted to one British political party, but more generally diffused throughout the British political and administrative establishment'.

Leaders from Attlee to Major have been tested by European 'problems'. Their difficulties relate to the problem of leading parties whose composition reflects the ambivalent attitudes of many British people to the post-war position. Britons are caught between the desire to hold on to country's past greatness and traditions (what former Foreign Secretary Douglas Hurd has called 'punching above its weight'), and yet also to keep apace with the modern world. Although most MPs recognise that the country has a European future, a number of them do not enthuse about the prospect.

Other countries, lacking the same attachments as Britain, do not experience the same feelings, or at least not to the same extent. As one former Conservative MP, Sir Anthony Meyer, put it: 'For France, Europe offers a chance to extend its influence; for Britain, Europe is a damage-limitation exercise'.

Dr Kaiser, as quoted above, offers[11] an interesting explanation from a continental perspective of the British predicament in Europe. He notes the lack of British experience of working as equal partners:
It is not only...a matter of having lost an empire without finding a role. More fundamentally, Britain had little experience of multilateral relationships conducted on equal terms. Its key external circles of influence after 1945 were characterised by clear hierarchies: Britain led the Commonwealth and Empire, and it was led by the United States. There was no clear European hierarchy, and the Foreign Office remained fixated by an outmoded 'balance-of-power' mentality which failed to take account of the strengthening Franco-German alliance.

Policy in Europe: a reflection

Inevitably, any assessment of British policy must dwell more on the performance of past administrations than of the present one. These are still early days in Labour's handling of European affairs, and comments on the performance of current ministers must remain tentative. However, discussion of the handling of earlier episodes does help to provide a focus on the problems which beset the British relationship with Europe, and highlights any trends in the way in which events tend to be managed.

Policy in the 1990s
British policy often seemed to be beset by contradictions. Conservative ministers frequently denounced interference or 'meddling' from Brussels bureaucrats on matters such as the environment, immigration or worker protection, and yet wanted to see more Union action on matters such as animal welfare. They made Brussels the scapegoat for the failure to achieve effective reform in the row over the export of live animals to the continent.

The last government was reluctant to see any further power handed over to European institutions. Its members tended to resist further majority voting, and clung to the national veto as a means of protecting sovereignty. However, the veto, as its name implies, is a negative tactic which may seem appropriate if policy is about obstructing measures which are unpalatable. But it does also mean that there are problems when you cease to be an opposer and become a proposer. Martin Kettle has pointed out[12] that:

Britain has no veto that other nations do not have, and therefore we remain just as vulnerable to the veto over things we want to do as we currently expect the others to be over things we don't...The British veto sounds fine until you realise that it also means a Greek veto.

Over the live animal row, Britain was looking for allies among other European governments, and it was only by creating such alliances that a compromise could be reached. Some countries from Southern Europe would have liked to have been able to use a veto to block such progress, but because of majority voting a solution was found.

By resisting an extension of powers to the European Parliament, ministers lost potential support from MEPs who consistently voted for the type of policies of which Britain often approves. A majority normally supported a crackdown on Union waste and fraud, opening up markets to Eastern Europe and reform of the CAP, all issues on which Britain was in the forefront.

The contradictory nature of British policy was apparent in its position over agriculture. The government wanted reform of the Common Agricultural Policy and to enlarge the Union to the East, a policy which makes such reform ever-more-urgent. But at the same time ministers were determined to resist an extension of majority voting. Yet if each state does retain its national veto, the task of achieving fundamental agrarian reform becomes all the more difficult.

This seems like short term thinking, and opponents of the Conservatives suggested that the country was left exposed and isolated in the Union by the way in which a series of events were handled. British interests and those of other European states sometimes coincide, but by failing to work with those nations we surrendered the chance to make progress on those close to British thinking. This isolation was exhibited in the crisis over mad cow disease (see p53-55).

Of course, it does require some boldness to accept the extension of majority voting which would make the enlarged Union work more efficiently, and which will become more necessary as the number of member states increases. It also requires a willingness to respect the prevailing view when it goes against you. However, rather than go along with the tide of European opinion, British ministers have in the past tended to play the nationalist card with bravura and portray Brussels as the enemy whose ploys must be resisted.

There were echoes of this approach in the Blair Government's reaction to the comments of the former German chancellor Oscar Lafontaine, over tax harmonisation (see box p.158-159). His initiative, supported by other spokespersons in the new German Government, offered a slice of candour of just the type from which John Major suffered routinely, and which Margaret Thatcher tended to relish. Both Tony Blair and Gordon Brown made it clear that they would use the veto to reject any attempts to harmonise or expand taxes; they would not allow British ministers to be overruled on taxation issues. Not for the first time in Britain's turbulent relations with its continental partners, ministers were forced onto the defensive as France and Germany seemed to be racing ahead towards another distant Euro-goal. That drive towards integration has been a consistent one ever since the two countries buried their national differences back in the 1950s, even if there have been periods when it has been placed on the back-burner.

Most people recognise that Britain cannot separate itself from the European fold, but within it ministers sometimes seem to find it difficult to find ways of making the Union work to the national advantage. By resisting the initiatives which other nations want in so many areas, it then becomes harder to achieve those goals that really matter to Britain. Yet by going along with them, ministers risk having their actions savaged in the Euro-sceptic tabloid press. It is difficult for even a pro-European administration to be a constructive, if distinctive, actor on the continental stage.

The Centre-Left in power in Europe: differing visions?

The arrival in power of a new German Government seemed like good news for the British Government of Tony Blair. Gerhard Schroder, the Social Democratic Chancellor, has displayed personal warmth for Tony Blair and his New Labour project, having in his election campaign talked of the prospect of Britain being offered an equal place in the Franco-German axis at the heart of the European Union, making it into a triangle. The two men seemed to share a common approach and a similarity of personal style and appeal.

By the end of 1998, the Centre-Left was in office in almost every EU state. 13 governments were broadly agreed on a programme to boost growth and cut unemployment through concerted state action, whereas the British and Spanish Administrations were suspicious of the direction in which continental leaders were heading. Europe's balance of power was shifting, and although the Blair Government was pleased to see a leftist preponderance among Union governments, it was soon uneasy about some developments being recommended.

Tony Blair's Third Way had been centre-stage in the political debates of the early period of his administration, but the plans of Oskar Lafontaine and the French socialist government seemed by comparison to be more akin to Old Labour. The French were talking about a cut to a 35 hour week and a major programme of state intervention to make economies grow. There was a form of expansionist Keynesianism underlying their proposals, the sort of policy that has been out of fashion in Britain for two decades.

The two positions of the Third Way and New European Way are not totally at variance, for both projects share certain characteristics, including a commitment to free trade, financial liberalisation and globalisation; there is also a fairly general acceptance of the importance of sound money. What distinguishes the two is the emphasis in the Leftist viewpoint on boosting public investment; adherents are concerned that the European Central Bank should show a greater concern for the social impact of its policies as it sets out interest rate policies.

The Third Way (Blair/Schroder)	The New European Way (Lafontaine/Left)
Sound money, e.g., low inflation, tight budgetary control	No fines for countries which run excessive budget deficits
Welfare to work, and flexible working practices	Massive boost to growth and jobs
Caution over economic /financial changes	Less secrecy in meetings, e.g., of Central Bank
Freedom of each country to determine its own tax policy.	Bold policy of tax harmonisation

The row over tax harmonisation: a case study

Oskar Lafontaine emphasised his commitment to tax harmonisation. Shortly before the Vienna Summit, the German minister outlined his plans to harmonise VAT levels, and to bring corporate taxes into line; he was even reported to have added income tax to his wish list. The German Chancellor, Herr Schroder, backed him on the issue, arguing that 'it is sensible in a single market with a single currency to have better tax coordination'. The Single Market Commissioner joined in too, and argued for extending harmonisation to energy and excise duties, among other taxes.

The French and German governments publicly committed themselves to making 'rapid progress towards tax harmonisation in Europe', and the display of solidarity among leading EU figures provoked serious disagreement between New Labour and the continental socialists. Oskar Lafontaine broadened the onslaught by arguing for an end to the unanimity rule, for in his view the national veto was no longer viable:

It is clear that as the Union enlarges, we cannot discuss details every time under the principle of unanimity.

Gordon Brown, the British Chancellor, was unmoved, and his rejoinder was that harmonisation was unnecessary and undesirable. Moreover, it was not going to happen:

Tax proposals require unanimity, and a change to that requires a treaty change which requires unanimity.

The argument revealed the extent of Franco-German cooperation. The governments of the two countries have in the past always been the engine of Europe's construction, and their renewed accord undermined British hopes of using its relationship with the Schroder Administration to become a third partner. The danger for ministers was that Britain might again become isolated in Europe, something they wished to avoid at almost all costs. This fear was intensified by the seeming interest of the two continental governments in pressing ahead with harmonisation within the eleven Euro countries. If this happened, it might complicate British prospects of joining the Euro in the future. By the time Britain is ready, a harmonised European tax system could be a reality, and accepting it could become a condition of entry into the single currency.

The British tabloid press was vehement in its denunciation of the Lafontaine plans, and he soon became a 'European from hell' in the writing of several journalists. Knowing what he wanted, he seemed to relish a battle to get his way. Euro-sceptics were up in arms at the idea of seeing UK tax rates brought into line with those elsewhere in Europe, and portrayed the episode as a further sign that the Europeans were intent upon a further push to closer integration. They suggested that harmonisation would mean - among other things - dearer food and children's clothes, and higher business taxes which would deter inward investment. Overall, there would be a further surrender of sovereignty.

The reality of what was being proposed was less stark than it was portrayed. It was not a battle of Britain versus the rest, and some of the proposals (for instance, ending 85 tax-breaks, only 10 of which are in operation in the UK) would have little impact. Nor was it a one-way exercise, for harmonisation would result in lower excise taxes on alcohol and petrol. However, continental ministers were concerned about the distortion caused in a single market by allowing some countries to have differing tax systems and to tax at lower rates. The Germans, in particular, were worried that lower corporation tax in Belgium, Ireland and to a lesser extent the United Kingdom, would place them at a competitive disadvantage.

In the face of such hostility in the media to 'unwanted' European initiatives, the Blair Government fell back on its threat to use the veto. Instead of looking for areas on which there was broad agreement such as tackling tax evasion and tax havens, and talking about the need for unanimity, the reaction was to resist with a clear 'no'. The policy played well at home, but there were some continental politicians who thought that the British response was too reminiscent of that which they had seen from earlier administrations.

NB Oscar Lafontaine is no longer in office, having fallen out with the German Chancellor

The future

Further integration?

In the years immediately prior to the 1997 general election, Conservative ministers often claimed to detect a growing consensus in Europe that the time was not ripe for further integration, and felt that this was a sign that they were winning the argument over the future of the European Union. They sensed a general and increasing antipathy among the European peoples to the idea of handing over more power to Brussels, and this encouraged them in their belief that economic and monetary union would probably not come about for several years. Yet whilst there were practical difficulties about achieving such union, the majority of other states were committed and did eventually go ahead, determined as they were to maintain progress towards the sort of Union they wished to emerge.

Chancellor Kohl was insistent that the pace of European integration should not be set by those who wanted to advance more cautiously, or not at all. As he put it in February 1996:

The slowest ship in the convoy should not be allowed to determine its speed. If individual partners are not prepared or able to participate in certain steps towards integration, the others should not be denied the opportunity to move forward.

British ministers in the 1990s increasingly spoke of a Europe in which they could pick and choose the parts they favoured, a Europe 'a la carte' in which they sought allies with whom they could achieve those things that mattered to them. The difficulty was that when so many items on the agenda were unacceptable to London, then leaders in other capitals were likely to hesitate before helping the country to fulfil its own aspirations.

Many suggestions have been put forward for a future based on 'variable geometry', a model of integration in which the participating countries decide whether or not they should participate in a particular activity. The underlying idea is that all states would normally take part in a core of essential areas, but they would be free to move at a different pace on others. The danger is that if one or more countries such as Britain opt out of nearly all major initiatives, then the result will be a 'two-speed' or 'two-tier Europe' in which some countries move ahead to integration at a rapid pace, whilst others who do not wish to go so far or so quickly trail behind. Such a model of 'concentric circles', with an inner circle committed to the fast track and an outer one to slower progress, has disadvantages, not least for Union solidarity. It would also call into question the rights of all member states to have equal status in decision-making, and could have budgetary implications as well; the inner few might be reluctant to finance those states who were unwilling to move ahead at the faster rate.

John Major was once dismissive of a 'multi-faceted, multi-speed, multi-layered' Europe, and saw a danger in there being 'an exclusive hard core either of countries or of policies'. He came to embrace the notion of variable geometry, via which he envisaged different EU states co-operating on varying aspects of common interest: 'Diversity is not a weakness to be suppressed, it is a strength to be harnessed'. The phase sometimes used by British ministers was 'flexible integration', a more diplomatically worded variant of some prevailing ideas (see also p162-163 for further discussion of flexible approaches).

For Britain the danger of any approach based on different rates of progress is that it will be in the slow lane on all key issues. The fear is that if we do not belong to the advance guard, we will be sidelined, and lose any ability to influence events in Europe. Britain would not be 'at the heart of Europe'. The new British Government claims that it does not wish to be left behind, and it has shown less enthusiasm for any variant of variable geometry. Its rhetoric implies that the intention is to join the Euro 'when the time is right', and that it will seek to cooperate in other fields unless essential interests are at stake. But there is still always the possibility that the time 'will not be ripe' for the Euro, and that Britain will find itself resisting the thrust of integration in other areas favoured by the powerful Franco-German alliance which is usually in the vanguard of further progress.

A commentator in Le Monde stated[13] a common view in France that the two countries, France and Britain, start from different perspectives when they consider their place in Europe:
For France, being at the heart of Europe remains a necessity. For Great Britain, it is just one option. Europe, seen from London, is not an end in itself, but a means of attaining specific objectives at particular times.

Labour's commitment to integration
Tony Blair has argued for closer EU integration in some areas, but greater diversity in others such as education and health. In a speech in Paris during the British Presidency, he reassured his audience of his pro-European credentials: 'I happen to share the European idealism. I am by instinct internationalist...Britain's future lies in being full partners in Europe'. He spoke of the need to ensure that there was a political framework to match progress in other areas, and spelt out the need to make that framework more relevant and in touch with people's concerns across the Union. He also urged the need for decentralisation where possible, declaring 'Vive la subsidiarite'. In December 1998, at the Vienna Summit, he urged a common defence and foreign policy, and elaborated on his suggestion of a more integrated European military capability. In addition, he backed close coordination of economic and employment policies, the focus being on creating jobs.

Flexible forms of co-operation

The idea of a **two speed Europe (Europe á deux vitesses)** has been around in EC/EU circles for more than two decades. It recognises that not all member states are able or willing to move towards integration at the same pace. Therefore, a means needs to be devised to allow the most committed states to fulfil their ambitions, without them being held back by those travelling in the slower lane.

The assumption is that all wish to reach the same destination and achieve the same degree of integration. There is understanding that particular policies can be difficult for individual states for valid and acceptable reasons. Which countries proceed at which pace is a matter for discussion and agreement, and those involved in any new project may vary from case to case. The hope is that the more advanced countries will assist those who lag behind, as part of a recognition that whatever the problems all are aiming for the same federal goal.

Variable geometry is the term for an á la carte decision to participate or not participate in every EU policy. In practice, there may be a small number of core countries who are involved in all activities, and if there is such a group this could result in a two speed Europe. To avoid this, the Union has usually chosen to move into only those policy areas where there is agreement on the desirability of an integrated approach - an exception would be the double British opt-out negotiated at Maastricht.

The á la carte approach poses difficulties in what is meant to be a close Union. If a number of states join only in those actions which they perceive to be of direct benefit to their national interest, then the likelihood of co-operation over a broad front is reduced. However, in an enlarged EU it could be that such flexibility accords with reality. Variable geometry may be the only means by which the large Union can be made to work.

John Major supported the idea of a non-exclusive hard-core as part of the flexible future he wished to encourage. He may or may not have understood the distinction between the two concepts here discussed. But it is a significant one. The idea of a two speed or multi-speed approach is compatible with future integration, even if in practice some states never reach the ultimate destination. Variable geometry is not, unless the 'picking and choosing' is confined to a very few policy areas.

The British opt-outs, a two speed Europe and variable geometry are all devices which points towards growing flexibility in the EU. They are an attempt to deal with a situation in which some members need to press ahead more quickly, but feel frustrated by those who move with greater caution. Former Chancellor Kohl's remark (see p160) reflects the frustration of one committed European who wanted the Union to advance at a faster pace than that of the slowest ship in the convoy. His comment echoed prevailing thinking within his Christian Democrat

Party, as expressed in a paper[14] which drew attention to the existence of a 'hard core [of member states of the European Union] oriented to greater integration and closer co-operation'. The comment was a recognition of the obvious fact that the countries of Europe were beginning to move at different speeds.

Intergovernmentalism or supranationalism?

In the search for new structures in Europe after World War Two, Monnet disliked the intergovernmentalism of the OEEC which he believed[15] to be 'the opposite of the Community spirit'. He rejected 'mere cooperation', and urged the creation of 'new functional authorities that superseded the sovereignty of existing nation-states'. In his view, the sovereign nations of the past could no longer solve the problems of the day. They could not ensure their own progress or control their own future.

From the beginning, British ministers doubted the wisdom or desirability of the integration for which he aimed, and disliked the spirit of supranationalism which pervaded bodies such as the ECSC and the EEC. In many key areas from economic policy to defence, and from welfare to foreign affairs, key decisions are still taken by national governments, even if this is in some cases done after Euro-level consultation. Where decisions are taken by the EU, they are usually taken at European Council or Council of Ministers level, so that the leading representatives of each country can mount a sturdy defence of national interests. Most of these decisions are still taken on the basis of unanimity, and even where majority voting has been introduced there is always an initial search for agreement.

Yet there are important supranational characteristics as well. Decisions taken at European level have the force of law in member countries, and as we have seen European law is superior to domestic law. The Commission has the power to take decisions and particularly to issue regulations and directives which are binding on member countries. In Britain, this has serious implications for the doctrine of Parliamentary Sovereignty. Moreover, the growth of majority voting and the increasing powers of the European Parliament, though both in their infancy, nonetheless suggest that the element of supranationalism is on the increase.

The process of integration has not always been easy, nor the path smooth. There have at times been difficulties between the member states, and the conflict between national interest and the interests of Europe as a whole has posed particular difficulties for some countries. Yet the direction of movement has always been towards greater integration, a term which the dictionary describes as 'the harmonious combination of elements into a single whole'.

Intergovernmentalism and integration have been two key forces at work in the evolution of the Community, and now the Union. At different times over the last forty years, one set of ideas has gained the ascendancy, as different thinkers and statesmen have pressed their particular viewpoint. The dispute is still at the heart of the controversy within the Union about the way it has developed and the future direction it should take.

The notion of intergovernmentalism has been remarkably resilient, and at different moments it has asserted itself strongly - whether in the failure of the EDC, the British fight over its budgetary contributions or the Thatcherite declaration in the Bruges speech. Yet despite these attempts to safeguard national interests, the Union has not only established itself; it has moved more closely together. It is now at the point where fundamental decisions have to be taken about future development, the more so as enlargement to the East becomes a strong likelihood in the coming years.

Political union

'Anti-Europeans' fear closer political union, and the consequent loss of sovereignty involved. The goal of such union is one which has been played down by British Euro-philes. In the discussions surrounding entry into the EEC in 1973, the possibility of any erosion of national independence was played down, and in the House of Commons the then Prime Minister was categoric about the country's future status:
Joining the Community does not entail a loss of national identity or an erosion of essential national sovereignty.

In recent years, those who disapprove of the direction the Community/Union has taken tend to quote and re-quote such words, alleging that the politicians who took Britain into Europe did so on the basis of a false prospectus, and therefore committed a major deceit. They have researched similar observations, as when Edward Heath later added that 'these fears [that we shall sacrifice independence and sovereignty] are completely unjustified'.

It is difficult to see how a group of nations can agree on radical and irreversible changes in their economic and social organisation without there being a reduction in the sovereignty of individual countries. The compensation is an increase in power and influence - and hopefully prosperity - for the group as a whole. This was not often made clear at the start, and it is still often suggested by some supporters of the EU that political union can be fended off. Yet that was the original aim of those who formed the Coal and Steel Community, as they planned for the 'European federation which is indispensable to the cause of peace'. For 'pro-European' British statesmen, the answer can only be to accept that this route is inevitable, or as has tended to happen, to seek to stave off the hour by placing a spoke in the wheel as new initiatives are put forward by Brussels. This tends to upset a number of our continental partners for whom the route marked integration is the one they wish to take.

A Federal future?

Indeed, one of the most contentious issues concerning the future of the Union is the extent to which it moves in a federal direction. Whereas Mr Heath is a willing federalist ('the sooner the better'), Lady Thatcher takes a different view. She fears that a creeping federal system is being achieved without it being fully appreciated, and urges the need to halt this 'conveyor-belt to federalism'. In the eyes of many right-wing British politicians the word remains anathema, for they see ideas of federalism and national sovereignty as fundamentally incompatible.

Most Europeans, including the Commission, wanted Maastricht to commit the EC to a federal European union. In itself, it is a harmless label, the word cited in the constitution of the European People's Party, the grouping with which the British Conservatives have developed closer ties. Yet in Britain, the word has horrifying connotations to many Conservatives, for whom stopping the drift in that direction has long been an object of policy.

Britain gave federal constitutions to Australia and Canada, and has used the system elsewhere in the Commonwealth. Some experiments did not work well, as in the West Indies and Nigeria, whereas the first ones mentioned have been more successful. However, despite our willingness to use them elsewhere, federal solutions are clearly not seen as suitable for use by the Mother Country.

The Oxford Dictionary describes the meaning of 'federal' as 'an association of units that are largely independent' and 'a system of government in which several states unite under a central authority but remain independent in internal affairs'. As such, it is designed to allow the maximum devolution of decision-making possible consistent with the needs of a workable union. No-one was seeking to see the Australians governed mainly from Canberra, but to give the advantages of common action on major issues whilst fully satisfying and respecting local traditions.

The replacement term in the Maastricht Treaty is apparently more to the liking of the Government; it is the 'ever closer union' formula which is to be found in the Treaty of Rome. Yet this seems to have more far-reaching implications, for it implies a never-ending journey in which supporters seek ultimately to merge their identities. 'Federal' at least has an end in view, for it involves a division of functions between the centre and the individual member-states. It also allows for the notion of 'subsidiarity', the idea that decisions should be taken at a local level wherever this is feasible.

The point was well made[16] in an editorial in 1991 of the Agence Europe. It noted that the phrasing of the Treaty of Rome
is far more menacing, to anyone concerned with preserving national sovereignty than a 'federal union'. An ever closer union must mean, if it means anything, that no matter how far we have gone in linking the member states to each other we must strive to go further still. A federal union, by contrast, usually means one in which the respective spheres of competence of the Union and its component parts are defined in a manner intended to be permanent.

The difficulty is that the word federal has assumed a significance out of all relation to what it really means. The media, especially the popular press, have often used it in the way that some Conservatives do, as if it implied the removal of power from the nation-state to some super-state. It is seen as denoting a move to centralisation and deeper integration so that MPs pounce on any proposal from the Commission suspecting that it brings the dreaded 'f' word ever-nearer.

Visions of the future; varying scenarios

Federalism

Federalism is a powerful but elusive concept, the more so as it tends to mean different things in Britain and on the continent. A federal structure is a form of government in which a constitution distributes powers between a central government and a series of states, giving substantial functions to each. Federations exist in Australia, Canada, Germany and the USA.

The trend in countries such as the United States over the past sixty years has been for more power to be taken at the centre, i.e. in Washington. This enables British politicians to portray federalism as involving increasingly centralised government.

On the continent, federalism, implies the opposite, decentralisation and subsidiarity. Subsidiarity enshrines the idea that power should only be exercised centrally if the central body can take action more effectively than the member states.

Confederalism

In a confederation, by a constitutional compact sovereign nations create a central government but limit its competence. The central government may make regulations for the constituent governments (i.e., states) but it exists and operates only at their direction - rather in the way that under the Articles of Confederation, the thirteen Southern states operated during the American Civil War.

If Federalism, as popularly understood in Britain involves a strong centre (Brussels) and weak states, a confederal structure is the opposite, providing for strong, dominant national governments and a weaker centre. Such a pattern, applied to the EU would allow for more emphasis to be placed on intergovernmentalism.

Increasingly, the talk among writers on the European Union is of 'variable geometry', and twin or multi-track structures, as explained in the box on p162-163. This envisages that the countries of Europe will move ahead at different speeds, and that an inner core of the Union will be more tightly integrated whilst an outer tier or tiers will move more slowly.

On the continent, the term arouses no such anxieties, for it implies quite the opposite. To a German, the notion of subsidiarity (which assumed so much importance in John Major's thinking at the time of Maastricht) presupposes the idea of a federal European state. It is the very essence of federalism, with a division of power between the different layers of government, European, national and regional.

The word has become a slogan for all that those who fear the drift of events in the Union. In denying its use, they are not only rejecting the formal structure of a fully-fledged federal European state, but all the moves such as the single currency, the stronger European institutions and the increasing search for a common approach to many matters of policy. As Hugo Young noted[17],

to be a 'fed' is merely to be on the pro-Union side of the argument. To be against the 'federal', is to propose oneself as a valiant upholder of the unchanging nation-state.

Clearly, Maastricht and other recent developments have moved the Union in the direction of more common policies. The general flow of events is to allow the EU more power in fields as diverse as defence and foreign policy, monetary union and the environment, for the 'entire thrust is towards...consensual action on the basis of majority-voting'. In a general sense, therefore, federalism is already with us, but in the exact meaning of the term, the creation of a new system of government, it is a long way off. No-one is actually seriously proposing it as a practical possibility at the present time. Indeed, as Andrew Marr has pointed out[18] 'Europe is a sprawling collection of states and cultures however economically close...some sort of settlement based on a loose federation is far likelier than the super-state feared by Germanophobes'.

An enlarged Europe?

Many states wish to join the European Union, among them several of the recently-created democracies of Central and Eastern Europe. Four enlargements have occurred already since 1957, indicating that the EU has been and remains a powerful magnet. Expansion to include applicant countries has several possible advantages. It will strengthen the EU by increasing its attraction as an export market for non-Union countries, it will enable the organisation to speak with a larger voice in world affairs, and it will help to increase stability on the continent, by promoting prosperity among the new states.

The French and the Germans have been keen to see further integration before further enlargement, although they accept the desirability of the latter. The British under John Major were keen to see substantial widening, hoping that this was a viable alternative to any deepening of existing Union bonds. Britain still firmly supports the idea of a larger EU, and at Amsterdam it was agreed that negotiations with a number of aspirant countries should be undertaken. Robin Cook, as Foreign Secretary, has argued strongly for an expanded Europe, and sees a need to bridge the wealth divide which characterises the continent in the post-Cold War world. He does not want to see a 'fortress of wealthy countries with the poor at its gate', an echo of past Labour objections to the European Community as a 'rich man's club'. He suggests that an enlarged EU can generate real transfers of wealth to the East, the benefits being that this will met the demands of social justice and reduce the threat of conflict on Europe's periphery.

If there is any chance of Europe managing the process of widening and deepening at the same time, it may be that an approach which enables different members to develop at different speeds is the only one that will cater for this. What is unlikely is that the hope of past Conservative ministers of preventing further deepening by supporting widening will work. Past history suggests that those committed to the latter have also been determined to maintain their commitment to the former.

The 'widening or deepening' debate is one which is set to continue, for the early pioneers were convinced of the importance of further European integration. Some critics of that vision, however, would argue that it has lost its relevance today. It may have been right for the time, but it is wrong for the world of the mid 1990s - the whole pattern of European politics has undergone such a profound change.

A changing Europe

Some writers and politicians have argued that the entire existence of the European Community was based on the Cold War which began within a few years of the ending of the 'real war' in 1945. They suggest that a strongly united Western Europe was highly relevant in the face of possible Soviet aggression, but that circumstances have changed following the downfall of communism and Soviet control. In the era of the Cold War a preoccupation with deepening the bonds between all of the member states was understandable and perhaps inevitable. It is not so self-evidently justifiable in a very different Europe which is soon likely to embrace states of contrasting stages of development.

Current and possible applications for membership: a summary

Country

EFTA countries	Latvia	
Iceland	Lithuania	
Liechtenstein	Macedonia	
Norway	Moldova	
	Poland*	
Central and	Romania	*NB **i** Only Morocco has ever*
East European Countries	Russia	*been turned down as an*
Albania	Slovakia	*applicant, on grounds that it*
Bosnia	Slovenia*	*does not qualify as a*
Bulgaria	Ukraine	*European country **ii** Post*
Byelorus		*Amsterdam (1997), the six*
Croatia	*Miscellaneous*	*asterisked countries are*
Czech Republic*	Cyprus*	*currently negotiating entry.*
Estonia*	Malta	*Their membership would add*
Hungary*	Turkey	*some 63m citizens, taking the*
		Union to 21 countries and
		nearly 435m peoples.

The six applicant countries began the process of negotiation more than two years ago. They are unlikely to be admitted before 2002, and far from speeding up · negotiations seem to be currently 'bogged down' in detail. They have to accept all of Europe's regulations, but in the case of the Poles and Slovenes are fearful that Germans and Italians may be able to move in and buy up their cheap land.

As for other aspirants, the time-scale has appeared discouraging. Countries such as Albania and Macedonia which at one time received sympathetic hints from Brussels (in return for taking Kosovan refugees in vast numbers) can at best hope only to get 'association agreements' in the coming near future. However, the new President of the Commission, Romano Prodi, is reported[20] as wanting to show a greater sense of urgency about EU enlargement. He is said to have plans to start negotiations with more countries (Bulgaria, Latvia, Lithuania, Malta, Romania and Slovakia are considered to be the likely choices). Turkey too, as long as it improves its record on human rights, has the prospect of entry in the foreseeable future. These proposals constitute but part of a bold vision which aims to see the Union expand from 15 to 27 members (from the Atlantic coast of Ireland to the Black Sea, a zone of some 500m people) within the next decade or so. They could even extend to offering association agreements to Russia and the Ukraine, and perhaps even to the countries of North Africa. They would involve some loosening of the terms of membership and a rapid reform of European institutions to accommodate the accelerated expansion.

Martin Kettle has taken up[19] this line of thought. In a penetrating article, he has discerned five 'big ideas' on which the present European Union is being constructed:

- Cooperation in foreign and security policy to allow Europe to play a co-ordinated role in world affairs
- Convergence on a federalist political model based upon solidarity
- Convergence on a deregulated free market governed by a stability-orientated monetary policy
- Convergence around a network of social benefits, largely to mitigate the effects of the tight money policy
- Enlargement to take in all nations, of whatever size, west of Russia.

He points out that - other than the tiny Benelux states - none of The Fifteen are committed to all of these goals. Britain may be particularly lukewarm, but others lack enthusiasm for some of them. In such a situation, 'in an internally unequal Europe, a variable geometry solution is not so much an option as an inevitability', and that the 'push to the East is making it so'.

It is not only the ending of the Cold War which has been the catalyst for change in Europe. But that was an important factor in forcing the nations of the Union to think again about the European project in a new way so that they are collectively equipped to cope with a new agenda. The European Union has already produced substantial benefits, primarily in keeping the peace in Western Europe, consolidating democracy and contributing to general prosperity. The challenges for the future are to continue to do those things, but also to create a Union which can win the wholehearted consent of its diverse peoples, one which is free, strong and united in its determination to bring such benefits to all those who live within the continent.

Conclusion

The story of British relations with the continent is inevitably unfinished. The process of European integration is ongoing, and Britain's long-term approach over the coming years under a different set of ministers is difficult to foresee. On past performance, it has been resolutely pragmatic, the emphasis being on the search for national advantage. This has inevitably involved ministers in what one writer calls[21] 'a more or less confrontational stance within a Community to which, it was [often] asserted, nothing significant had been surrendered'.

Yet by signing the Treaty of Rome, Britain did bind itself to what was always a potentially federalist organisation. This was relatively unimportant when federalist feelings were kept 'under wraps' - for instance, in the 1970s when there were other preoccupations - but it is more important when the drive towards integration is back on the agenda. As Young has expressed[22] the situation:

The integrationist thrust...is the likely long-term course of history. It has, with stops and starts, been the thrust of the last 20 years. The prophets of impasse have proved false, the prophets of evolution correct.

References

Chapter one - Post-war cooperation in Europe, 1945-1973

1. Hugo Young, This Blessed Plot, Macmillan, 1998.
2. Jean Monnet, Memoirs, Doubleday and Co., New York, 1978.
3. Walter Hallstein, *European Community*, February 1966
4. Archbishop of York, *Federal Union News*, 23 December 1939.
5. Labour Party document, European Unity, May 1950.
6. As in 1 above.
7. As in 1 above.
8. As in 1 above.
9. Dr L Robins, *Talking Politics*, Spring 1997.
10. F Duchene, 'More or Less than European? European Integration in Retrospect', in C Crouch and D Marquand, The Politics of 1992, *Political Quarterly*, 1993 Blackwell.
11. P Ludlow, Historical Aspects of Britain's Relationship with Europe, Paper delivered to PSA Conference, 1996.

Chapter two - Britain and the European Community: from entry to Maastricht

1. H Wilson, Speech in the House of Commons Debate, 1975.
2. R Jenkins, European Diary 1977-1981, Collins, 1989.
3. M Thatcher, The Downing Street Years, Harper Collins, 1993.
4. As quoted in 3 above.
5. As quoted in 3 above.
6. Dr L Robins, *Talking Politics*, Spring 1997.
7. *The Independent*, 8 November, 1990.

Chapter three - From Maastricht to Amsterdam

1. Quoted in C Pilkington, Issues in British Politics, Macmillan, 1998.
2. D Butler and M Westlake, British Politics and the European Elections 1994, Macmillan, 1995.

Chapter four - EU institutions

1. J Monnet, Memoirs, Doubleday and Co., New York, 1978.
2. M Holland, European Integration: From Community to Union, Pinter, 1994.
3. Sir L Brittan, Making Law in the European Union, Paper delivered to Centre for Legislative Studies, University of Hull, March, 1994.
4. Prof. P Norton, *Talking Politics*, Spring 1995.
5. P Ashdown, Speech to Centre for European Reform, 16 July 1998.
6. R Cook, Interview in *New Statesman*, August 13 1998.
7. Demos, Rebranding Europe, 1998.

Chapter five - The impact of the EU on government and politics

1. Prof. P Norton, *Talking Politics*, Spring 1995.
2. As in 1 above.

Chapter six - Political parties and Europe

1. W Hague, Speech in Fontainebleau, 19 May 1998.
2. S Bulmer, 'Britain and European Integration', Politics UK, Prentice Hall, 1998.

Chapter seven - Pressure groups and popular opinion

1. W Grant, Pressure Groups, Politics and Democracy in Britain, Harvester Wheatsheaf, 1995.
2. R Baggott, Pressure groups today, MUP, 1995.

Chapter eight - Some EU policies and their impact on Britain

1. N Nugent, The Government and Politics of the European Union, Macmillan, 1994.
2. *The Guardian*, 18.4.1998.
3. *The Guardian*, 20.7.1999.
4. *The Guardian*, 18.3.1999.

Chapter nine - The balance sheet of Britain's membership

1. T Blair, *The Sunday Times*, 5.5.1996.
2. A Turner, as in 1 above.
3. As in 2 above.
4. N Lamont, as in 1 above.

Chapter ten - Britain and Europe: the past and the future

1. Hugo Young, This blessed Plot, Macmillan, 1998.
2. Sir A Eden, as quoted in Britain and European Cooperation Since 1945, S Greenwood, Blackwell, 1992.
3. FS Northedge, Descent From Power: British Foreign Policy 1945-73, Allen and Unwin, 1974.
4. As in 1 above.
5. G Martin, Head of European Commission office in London, as quoted in British Politics and Europe, A Davies, Hodder and Stoughton, 1998.
6. A Adonis, The Observer, 17 November, 1996.
7. W Kaiser, Using Europe, Abusing the Europeans, as quoted in 6 above.
8. Lord Tebbit, as quoted in 6 above.
9. As in 6 above.
10. D Butler and M Westlake, British Politics and the European Elections 1994, Macmillan, 1995.
11. W Kaiser, as in 6 above.
12. M Kettle, *The Guardian*, 22.9.1995.
13. Le Monde, as quoted in 12 above.
14. Reflections on European Policy, Christian Democrat Study Paper, Sept 1994.
15. J Monnet, Memoirs, Doubleday and Co., New York, 1978.
16. Agence Europe, 1991, as quoted by H Young, *The Guardian*, 10.9.1991.
17. H Young, as in 15.
18. A Marr, *The Observer*, 10.1.1999.
19. M Kettle, *The Guardian*, 5.11.1994.
20. S Bates, *The Guardian*, 14.10.1999.
21. As in 2 above.
22. Hugo Young, as in 15 above.

Further reading

Many of the books on the European Union are written at a very advanced level, and they are too obscure or theoretical for students requiring an introduction to the subject. **Introducing the European Union** (available from the Politics Association) and written by the author of this book, seeks to remedy this deficiency of appropriate literature, and is an accessible account. A standard text is that by S George, **Politics and Policy in the European Community** (OUP, 1996), but this is now rather dated. More recent is Neill Nugent's **The Government and Politics of the European Union** (Macmillan, 1999), a very comprehensive account for reference purposes. S Henig, **The Uniting of Europe** (Routledge, 1997) is a shorter, but interesting account of the development of the Union, and it deals with British involvement at key points in the unfolding story. Timothy Bainbridge's **The Penguin Companion to European Union** (1998) is an invaluable survey of the ideas, institutions and personalities which have been influential in the evolution of the EC/EU.

For Britain and Europe, Hugo Young's vast recent survey, **This Blessed Plot** (Macmillan, 1998) provides a fascinating review of the subject of British relations with the continent in the post-war era, but for most candidates it is to be delved into, rather than read line by line. Colin Pilkington's **Britain in the European Union Today** (MUP 1995) is a manageable, interesting and useful review. The recent study by Alan Davies (a Chief Examiner on Europe) **British Politics and Europe** (Hodder and Stoughton, 1998) is brief, intelligent and easily readable; it seeks to examine Britain's participation in, and relationship to, the European Union. Short but erudite is the volume by Sean Greenwood in the Historical Association Studies series, **Britain and European Cooperation Since 1945**.

In addition to the above, students are advised to look out for articles in the *Politics Review* and *Talking Politics*, as well as in journals such as *The Economist* and *The New Statesman*. Reading of the broadsheet press is illuminating, *The Guardian, The Independent* and *The Observer* adopting a broadly pro-European stance, whilst *The Times* and *The Daily Telegraph* are more Euro-sceptical.

Index